INTRODUCTION

Distinctive Home Designs

This collection includes the best selling small and narrow lot home plans from some of the nation's leading designers and architects. Only quality plans with sound design, functional layout, energy efficiency and affordability have been selected.

This plan book covers a wide range of architectural styles in a popular range of sizes. A broad assortment is presented to match a wide variety of lifestyles and budgets. Each design page features floor plans, a front view of the house, and a list of special features. All floor plans show room dimensions, exterior dimensions and the interior square footage of the home.

◆

Technical Specifications

Every effort has been made to ensure that these plans and specifications meet most nationally recognized building codes (BOCA, Southern Building Code Congress and others). Drawing modifications and/or the assistance of a local architect or professional designer are sometimes necessary to comply with local codes or to accommodate specific building site conditions.

◆

Detailed Material Lists

An accurate material list showing the quantity, dimensions, and description of the major building materials necessary to construct your new home can save you a considerable amount of time and money. See Home Plans Index on page 82 for availability.

◆

Blueprint Ordering - Fast and Easy

Your ordering is made simple by following the instructions on page 83. See page 82 for more information on what type of blueprint packages are available and how many plans sets to order.

◆

Your Home, Your Way

The blueprints you receive are a master plan for building your new home. They start you on your way to what may well be the most rewarding experience of your life.

DREAM HOMES
PRESENTS

Small & Narrow Lot
HOME PLANS

CONTENTS

House shown on front cover is Plan #556-0203 and is featured on page 20

Small And Narrow Lot Home Plans is published by Home Design Alternatives, Inc. (HDA, Inc.) 4390 Green Ash Drive, St. Louis, MO 63045. All rights reserved. Reproduction in whole or in part without written permission of the publisher is prohibited. Printed in U.S.A © 1999. Artist drawings shown in this publication may vary slightly from the actual working blueprints.

How You Can Customize Our Plans Into Your Dream Home

Many of the plans in this book are customizable through the use of our exclusive Customizer Kit™. Look for this symbol on the plan pages for availability.

With the Customizer Kit you have unlimited design possibilities available to you when building a new home. It allows you to alter virtually any architectural element you wish, both on the exterior and interior of the home. The Kit comes complete with simplified drawings of your selected home plan so that you can sketch out any and all of your changes. To help you through this process, the Kit also includes a workbook called "The Customizer," a special correction pen, a red marking pencil, an architect's scale and furniture layout guides. These tools, along with HDA's customizer drawings, allow you to experiment with various design changes prior to having a design professional modify the actual working drawings.

Before placing your order for blueprints consider the type and number of changes you plan to make to your selected design. If you wish to make only minor design changes such as moving interior walls, changing window styles, or altering foundation types, we strongly recommend that you purchase reproducible masters along with the Customizer Kit. These master drawings, which contain the same information as the blueprints, are easy to modify

because they are printed on erasable, reproducible paper. Also, by starting with complete detailed drawings, and planning out your changes with the Customizer Kit, the cost of having a design professional or your builder make the required drawing changes will be considerably less. After the master drawings are altered, multiple blueprint copies can be made from them.

If you anticipate making a lot of changes, such as moving exterior walls and changing the overall appearance of the house, we suggest you purchase only one set of blueprints as a reference set and the Customizer Kit to document your desired changes. When making major design changes, it is always advisable to seek out the assistance of an architect or design professional

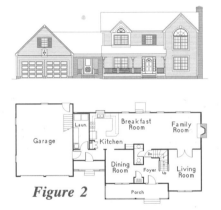

Figure 2

Figure 3

to review and redraw that portion of the blueprints affected by your changes.

Typically, having a set of reproducible masters altered by a local designer can cost as little as a couple hundred dollars, whereas redrawing a portion or all of the blueprints can cost considerably more depending on the extent of the changes. Like most projects, the more planning and preparation you can do on your own, the greater the savings to you.

Finally, you'll have the satisfaction of knowing that your custom home is uniquely and exclusively yours.

Examples of Customizing

Thousands of builders and home buyers have used the HDA Customizer Kit to help them modify their home plans, some involving minor changes, many with dramatic alterations. Examples of actual projects are shown here.

Figure 1 shows the front elevation and first floor plan for one of HDA's best-selling designs.

Figure 2 shows how one plan customer made few but important design changes such as completely reversing the plan to better accommodate his building site; adding a second entrance for ease of access to the front yard from the kitchen; making provisions for a future room over the garage by allowing for a stairway and specifying windows in place of louvers, plus other modifications.

Figure 3 shows another example of an actual project where the design shown in Figure 1 was dramatically changed to achieve all of the desired features requested by the customer. This customized design proved to be so successful that HDA obtained permission to offer it as a standard plan.

Figure 1

BOONE

Spacious Dining And Living Areas

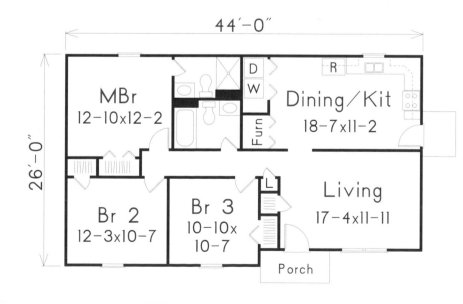

44'-0"

26'-0"

MBr
12-10x12-2

D
W

R

Dining/Kit
18-7x11-2

Furn

Br 2
12-3x10-7

Br 3
10-10x
10-7

L

Living
17-4x11-11

Porch

 Customize This Plan SEE PAGE 4

 Material List Available SEE PAGE 81

1,104 total square feet of living area

Special features

■ Master bedroom includes private bath

■ Convenient side entrance to kitchen/dining area

■ Laundry area located near kitchen

■ Large living area creates comfortable atmosphere

■ 3 bedrooms, 2 baths

■ Crawl space foundation, drawings also include basement and slab foundations

Price Code AA

Plan #556-0505

WOODFIELD

Dining With A View

1,524 total square feet of living area

Special features

- Delightful balcony overlooks two-story entry illuminated by oval window
- Roomy first floor master suite offers quiet privacy
- All bedrooms feature one or more walk-in closets
- 3 bedrooms, 2 1/2 baths, 2-car garage
- Basement foundation
- 951 square feet on the first floor and 573 square feet on the second floor

    Price Code B

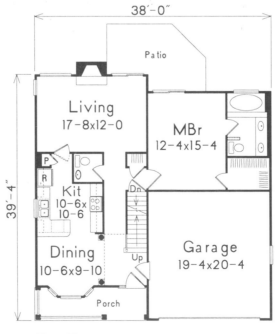

First Floor

Second Floor

 CUSTOMIZER KiT — Customize This Plan **SEE PAGE 4**

 MATERIAL LIST — Material List Available **SEE PAGE 81**

Plan #556-0652

DEXTER

Compact Home Yet Charming And Functional

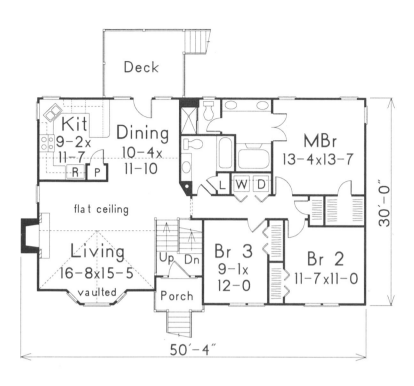

1,404 total square feet of living area

Special features

- Split foyer entrance
- Bayed living area features unique vaulted ceiling and fireplace
- Wrap-around kitchen has corner windows for added sunlight and a bar that overlooks dining area
- Master suite features a garden tub with separate shower
- Back deck provides handy access to dining room and kitchen
- 3 bedrooms, 2 baths, 2-car drive under garage
- Basement foundation, drawings also include partial crawl space foundation

Price Code A

CUSTOMIZER KiT Customize This Plan **SEE PAGE 4**

MATERIAL LIST $ Material List Available **SEE PAGE 81**

Plan #556-0176

BRIGHTMOORE

Functional Layout For Comfortable Living

1,360 total square feet of living area

Special features

- Kitchen/dining room features island work space and plenty of dining area
- Master bedroom with large walk-in closet and private bath
- Laundry room adjacent to the kitchen for easy access
- Convenient workshop in garage
- Large closets in secondary bedrooms
- 3 bedrooms, 2 baths, 2-car side entry garage
- Basement foundation, drawings also include crawl space and slab foundations

Price Code A

68'-0"

Patio

30'-0"

Garage
22-4x23-5

Kit/Din
17-6x14-6

MBr
12-9x14-6

work shop
10-8x6-0

Family
17-6x14-7

Br 3
12-1x11-3

Br 2
12-2x11-3

Covered Porch
23-0x8-0

 **CUSTOMIZER KiT** Customize This Plan **SEE PAGE 4**

 **MATERIAL LIST $** Material List Available **SEE PAGE 81**

Plan #556-0217

OAKBERRY

Quaint Country Home Is Ideal

| 1,028 total square feet of living area |

Special features

- Master bedroom conveniently located on first floor
- Well-designed bathroom contains laundry facilities
- L-shaped kitchen with handy pantry
- Tall windows flank family room fireplace
- Cozy covered porch provides unique angled entry into home
- 3 bedrooms, 1 bath
- Crawl space foundation
- 728 square feet on the first floor and 300 square feet on the second floor

Price Code AA

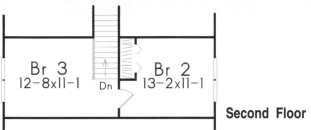

Br 3
12-8x11-1 Dn

Br 2
13-2x11-1

Second Floor

Br 1
10-0x
13-0

Up

Stor

Kitchen
13-2x12-4

W D

R

P

Family
15-10x13-0

Porch depth 8-0

30'-6"

30'-0"

First Floor

CUSTOMIZER KIT
Customize This Plan
SEE PAGE 4

MATERIAL LIST $
Material List Available
SEE PAGE 81

REDFIELD

Quaint Exterior, Full Front Porch

| 1,657 total square feet of living area |

Special features

- Stylish pass-through between living and dining areas
- Master bedroom is secluded from living area for privacy
- Large windows in breakfast and dining area
- 3 bedrooms, 2 1/2 baths, 2-car drive under garage
- Basement foundation
- 1,046 square feet on the first floor and 611 square feet on the second floor

Price Code B

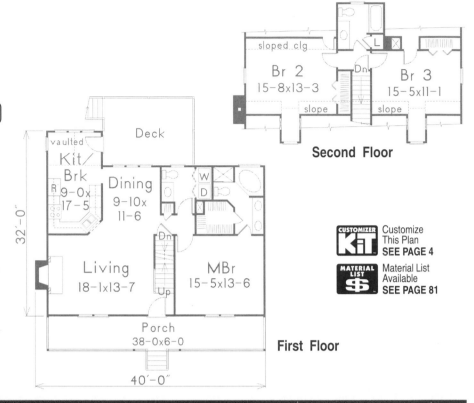

Second Floor

First Floor

CUSTOMIZER KiT — Customize This Plan **SEE PAGE 4**

MATERIAL LIST $ — Material List Available **SEE PAGE 81**

Plan #556-0174

To order blueprints use the form on page 00 or call 1 000 DREAM HOME (??? ????)

Vaulted Ceilings And Light Add Dimension

1,676 total square feet of living area

Special features

- The living area skylights and large breakfast room with bay window provide plenty of sunlight

- The master bedroom has a walk-in closet; the secondary bedrooms are accented with a circle-top window in one and large closets in both

- Vaulted ceilings, plant shelving and a fireplace provide a quality living area

- 3 bedrooms, 2 baths, 2-car garage

- Basement foundation, drawings also include crawl space and slab foundations

      Price Code B

Deck

MBr
15-1x14-4

sky lts

Living
18-10x19-1
vaulted

Dining
10-0x12-9

Kit/Brk
11-10x13-2

Dn

P | W D

Br 3
15-1x10-7
vaulted

plant sh.

Br 2
13-8x11-8

Foyer

Porch

Garage
21-5x24-0

43'-8"

64'-0"

 Customize This Plan SEE PAGE 4

 Material List Available SEE PAGE 81

Plan #556-0229

FARMVIEW

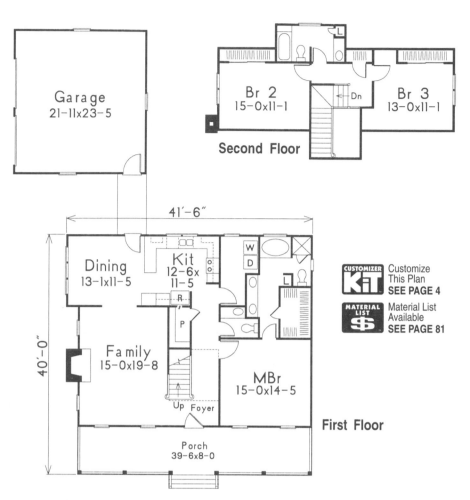

Second Floor

Garage
21-11x23-5

Br 2
15-0x11-1

Dn

Br 3
13-0x11-1

Dining
13-1x11-5

Kit
12-6x
11-5

W
D

41'-6"

40'-0"

Family
15-0x19-8

R

P

MBr
15-0x14-5

Up   Foyer

First Floor

Porch
39-6x8-0

CUSTOMIZER **KiT**   Customize
This Plan
SEE PAGE 4

MATERIAL LIST **$**   Material List
Available
SEE PAGE 81

Two-Story Foyer Adds Spacious Feeling

1,814 total square feet of living area

Special features

- Large master suite includes a spacious bath with garden tub, separate shower and large walk-in closet

- Spacious kitchen and dining areas brightened by large windows and patio access

- Detached 2-car garage with walkway leading to house adds to the charm of this country home

- Large front porch

- 3 bedrooms, 2 1/2 baths, 2-car detached garage

- Crawl space foundation, drawings also include slab foundation

- 1,288 square feet on the first floor and 526 square feet on the second floor

Price Code D

Plan #556-0201

ASHFIELD

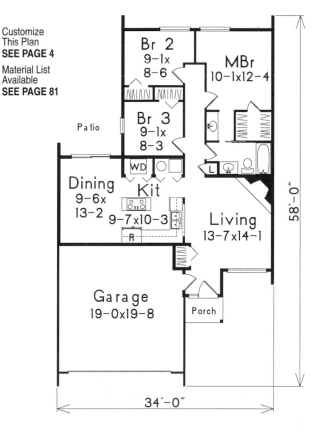

Customize This Plan **SEE PAGE 4**

Material List Available **SEE PAGE 81**

Easily Converts To Duplex Unit

1,044 total square feet of living area

Special features

- Great layout for narrow lot
- Master bedroom with walk-in closet, dressing area and private entrance to bath
- Convenient entrance from garage into main living area
- Kitchen includes island cook top, stackable washer/dryer closet and adjacent dining area with patio access
- Living room boasts cozy corner fireplace
- 3 bedrooms, 1 bath, 2-car garage
- Crawl space foundation

Price Code AA

Plan #556-0471

HOLLAND

Great Room Window Adds Character Inside And Out

1,368 total square feet of living area

Special features

- Entry foyer steps down to open living area which combines great room and formal dining area

- Vaulted master suite includes box bay window, large vanity, separate tub and shower

- Cozy breakfast area features direct access to the patio and pass-through kitchen

- Handy linen closet located in hall

- 3 bedrooms, 2 baths, 2-car garage

- Basement foundation

    Price Code A

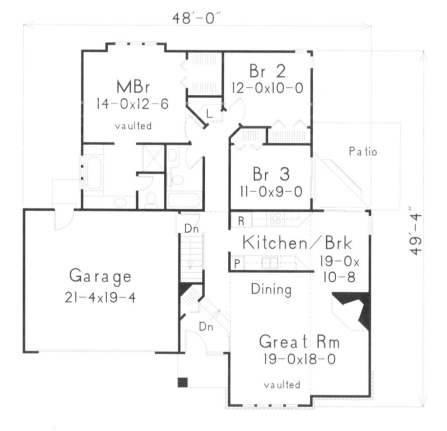

48'-0"

MBr
14-0x12-6
vaulted

Br 2
12-0x10-0

L

Patio

49'-4"

Br 3
11-0x9-0

R

Dn

Kitchen/Brk
19-0x
10-8

Garage
21-4x19-4

P

Dining

Dn

Great Rm
19-0x18-0

vaulted

CUSTOMIZER KiT Customize This Plan SEE PAGE 4

MATERIAL LIST $ Material List Available SEE PAGE 81

Plan #556-0271

Customize
This Plan
SEE PAGE 4

Material List
Available
SEE PAGE 81

Second Floor

Br 3
9-0x
11-0

Br 2
10-0x9-8

MBr
11-8x13-0

Dn

skylt   open to below

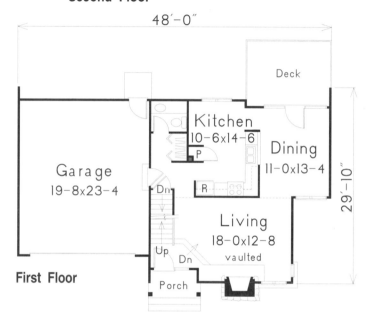

48'-0"

Deck

Kitchen
10-6x14-6

P

Dining
11-0x13-4

Garage
19-8x23-4

Dn

R

29'-10"

Living
18-0x12-8

Up

Dn   vaulted

First Floor

Porch

Exterior Accents Add Charm To This Cottage

1,359 total square feet of living area

Special features

- Lattice-trimmed porch, stone chimney and abundant windows lend outside appeal
- Spacious, bright breakfast area with pass-through to formal dining room
- Large walk-in closets in all bedrooms
- Extensive deck expands dining and entertaining area
- 3 bedrooms, 2 1/2 baths, 2-car garage
- Basement foundation
- 668 square feet on the first floor and 691 square feet on the second floor

Price Code A

Plan #556-0104

MAITLAND

Interesting Plan For Narrow Lot

(1,516 total square feet of living area)

Special features

- Spacious great room is open to dining with a bay and unique stair location
- Attractive and well-planned kitchen offers breakfast bar and built-in pantry
- Smartly designed master suite enjoys patio views
- 3 bedrooms, 2 baths, 2-car garage
- Basement foundation

    Price Code B

 Customize This Plan SEE PAGE 4    Material List Available SEE PAGE 81

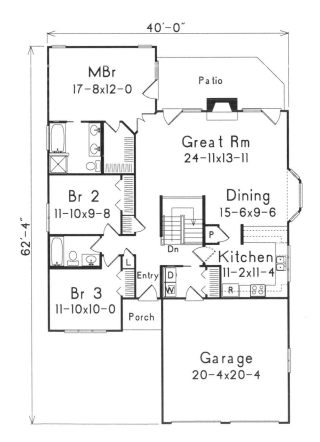

40'-0"

62'-4"

MBr 17-8x12-0

Patio

Great Rm 24-11x13-11

Br 2 11-10x9-8

Dining 15-6x9-6

Dn

P

Kitchen 11-2x11-4

Entry

L

D W

R

Br 3 11-10x10-0

Porch

Garage 20-4x20-4

Plan #556-0659

WOODHALL

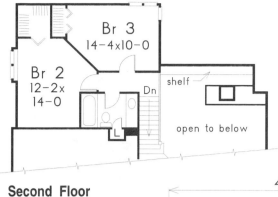

Second Floor

Br 3
14-4x10-0

Br 2
12-2x
14-0

shelf

Dn

L

open to below

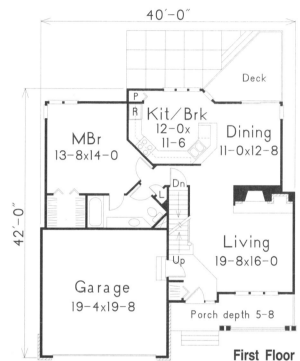

40'-0"

42'-0"

Deck

P
R

Kit/Brk
12-0x
11-6

Dining
11-0x12-8

MBr
13-8x14-0

Dn

L

Living
19-8x16-0

Up

Garage
19-4x19-8

Porch depth 5-8

First Floor

CUSTOMIZER KiT Customize This Plan **SEE PAGE 4**

MATERIAL LIST $ Material List Available **SEE PAGE 81**

Gabled Front Porch Adds Charm And Value

1,443 total square feet of living area

Special features

- Raised foyer and cathedral ceiling in living room
- Impressive tall-wall fireplace between living and dining rooms
- Open U-shaped kitchen with breakfast bay
- Angular side deck accentuates patio and garden
- First floor master bedroom suite has a walk-in closet and a corner window
- 3 bedrooms, 2 baths, 2-car garage
- Basement foundation
- 1,006 square feet on the first floor and 437 square feet on the second floor

Price Code A

Plan #556-0106

DORADO

Floor-To-Ceiling Window Expands Two-Story

1,246 total square feet of living area

Special features

- Corner living room window adds openness and light
- Out-of-the-way kitchen with dining area; back garden close by
- Private first-floor master bedroom with corner window
- Large walk-in closets are located on both floors
- Easily built perimeter allows economical construction
- 3 bedrooms, 2 baths, 2-car garage
- Basement foundation
- 846 square feet on the first floor and 400 square feet on the second floor

Price Code A

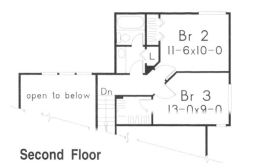

Second Floor

Br 2
11-6x10-0

open to below

Br 3
13-0x9-0

CUSTOMIZER KiT — Customize This Plan SEE PAGE 4

MATERIAL LIST $ — Material List Available SEE PAGE 81

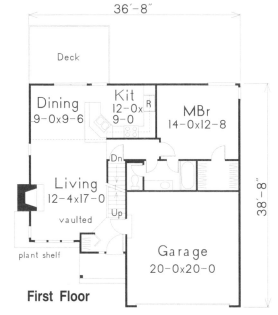

36'-8"

38'-8"

Deck

Dining
9-0x9-6

Kit
12-0x9-0

MBr
14-0x12-8

Living
12-4x17-0
vaulted

Garage
20-0x20-0

plant shelf

First Floor

Plan #556-0102

CUSTOMIZER **KiT** Customize This Plan SEE PAGE 4

MATERIAL LIST **$** Material List Available SEE PAGE 81

Well-Designed Plan Perfect For Entertaining

1,556 total square feet of living area

Special features

- Corner fireplace in living area warms surroundings
- Spacious master suite includes walk-in closet and private bath with double bowl vanity
- Compact kitchen designed for efficiency
- Covered porches in both front and back of home add coziness
- 3 bedrooms, 2 baths, 2-car attached carport
- Slab foundation

Price Code B

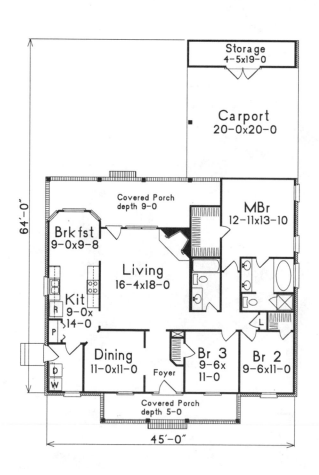

Storage
4-5x19-0

Carport
20-0x20-0

64'-0"

Covered Porch
depth 9-0

MBr
12-11x13-10

Brkfst
9-0x9-8

Living
16-4x18-0

Kit
9-0x
14-0

R

P

D
W

Dining
11-0x11-0

Foyer

Br 3
9-6x
11-0

Br 2
9-6x11-0

L

Covered Porch
depth 5-0

45'-0"

CEDARWOOD

Rambling Country Bungalow

> 1,475 total square feet of living area

Special features

- Family room features a high ceiling and prominent corner fireplace
- Kitchen with island counter and garden window makes a convenient connection between the family and dining rooms
- Private hallway leads to the three bedrooms, all with large walk-in closets
- Covered breezeway joins main house and garage
- Full width entry covered porch lends a country touch
- 3 bedrooms, 2 baths, 2-car garage
- Slab foundation, drawings also include crawl space foundation

Price Code B

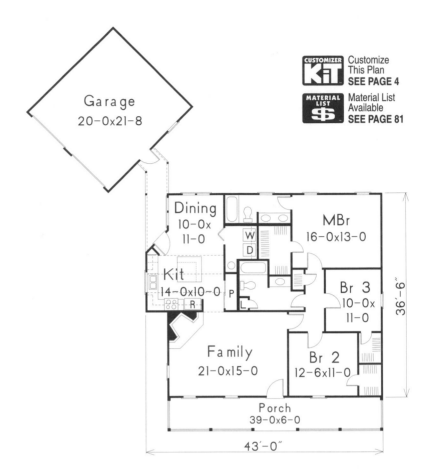

CUSTOMIZER KiT — Customize This Plan SEE PAGE 4

MATERIAL LIST $ — Material List Available SEE PAGE 81

Plan #556-0203

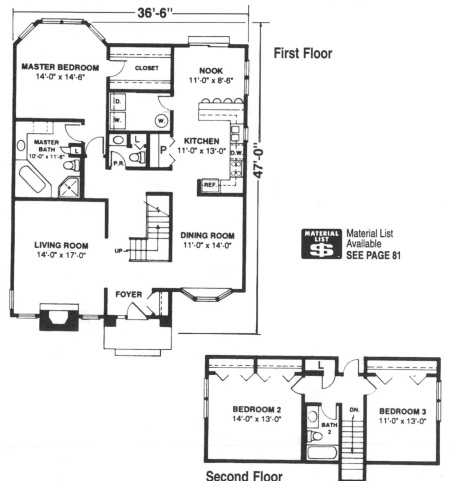

First Floor

36'-6"

MASTER BEDROOM
14'-0" x 14'-6"

CLOSET

NOOK
11'-0" x 8'-6"

D.

W.

W.

MASTER
BATH
10'-0" x 11'-6"

L

KITCHEN
11'-0" x 13'-0"

P

P.R.

D.W.

REF.

47'-0"

LIVING ROOM
14'-0" x 17'-0"

UP

DINING ROOM
11'-0" x 14'-0"

FOYER

MATERIAL LIST $ Material List Available **SEE PAGE 81**

BEDROOM 2
14'-0" x 13'-0"

L

DN.

BATH
2

BEDROOM 3
11'-0" x 13'-0"

Second Floor

Terrific Cottage-Style Design

1,992 total square feet of living area

Special features

- Master bedroom includes many luxuries such as an oversized private bath and large walk-in closet

- Kitchen area is spacious with a functional eat-in breakfast bar and is adjacent to nook perfect for breakfast room

- Plenty of storage is featured in both bedrooms on the second floor and in the hall

- Enormous utility room is centrally located on the first floor

- 3 bedrooms, 2 1/2 baths

- Basement foundation

- 1,403 square feet on the first floor and 519 square feet on the second floor

Price Code C

Plan #556-1297-1

CEDARVILLE

Plan #556-1216-1 partial basement/crawl space
Plan #556-1216-2 slab

Simply Country

1,668 total square feet of living area

Special features

- Simple but attractive styling ranch home is perfect for a narrow lot
- Front porch entrance opens into foyer that has coat closet
- Garage entrance to home leads to kitchen through mud room/laundry
- U-shaped kitchen opens to dining area and family room
- Three bedrooms are situated at the rear of the home with two full baths
- Master bedroom has walk-in closet
- 3 bedrooms, 2 baths, 2-car garage
- Basement/crawl space foundation or slab foundation drawings available, please specify when ordering

Price Code B

Material List Available
SEE PAGE 81

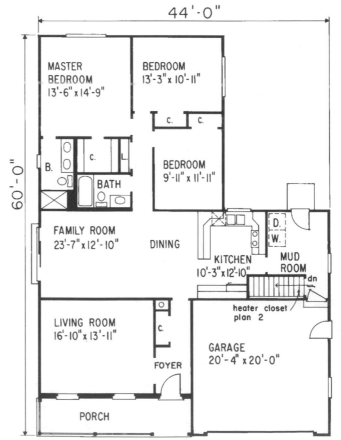

WAVERLY

Gabled, Covered Front Porch

1,320 total square feet of living area

Special features

- Functional U-shaped kitchen features pantry
- Large living and dining areas join to create open atmosphere
- Secluded master bedroom includes private full bath
- Covered front porch opens into large living area with convenient coat closet
- Utility/laundry room located near the kitchen
- 3 bedrooms and 2 baths
- Crawl space foundation

Price Code A

CUSTOMIZER KIT Customize This Plan **SEE PAGE 4**

MATERIAL LIST $ Material List Available **SEE PAGE 81**

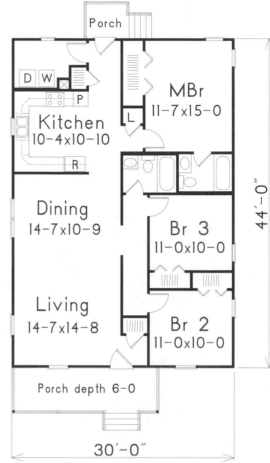

Porch

Kitchen 10-4x10-10

D W P

MBr 11-7x15-0

L

Dining 14-7x10-9

Br 3 11-0x10-0

Living 14-7x14-8

Br 2 11-0x10-0

R

Porch depth 6-0

44'-0"

30'-0"

Plan #556-0297

CRAWFORD

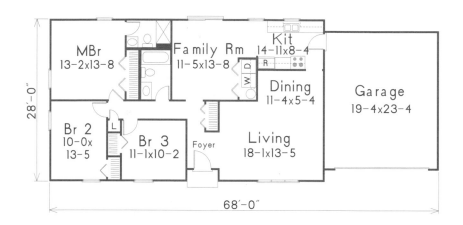

MBr
13-2x13-8

Family Rm
11-5x13-8

Kit
14-11x8-4

W D

R

Dining
11-4x5-4

Garage
19-4x23-4

28'-0"

Br 2
10-0x
13-5

L

Br 3
11-1x10-2

Foyer

Living
18-1x13-5

68'-0"

CUSTOMIZER KiT Customize This Plan **SEE PAGE 4**

MATERIAL LIST $$ Material List Available **SEE PAGE 81**

Roomy Ranch For Easy Living

1,343 total square feet of living area

Special features

- Separate and convenient family and living/dining areas
- Nice-sized master bedroom suite with large closet and private bath
- Foyer with convenient coat closet opens into combined living/dining room
- Kitchen has sliding door access to the outdoors
- 3 bedrooms, 2 bath, 2-car garage
- Crawl space foundation, drawings also include basement foundation

Price Code A

Plan #556-0200

PINEHURST I

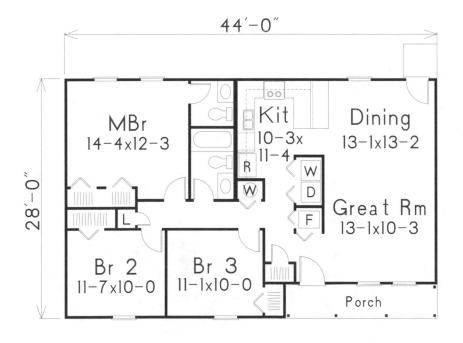

44'-0"

28'-0"

MBr
14-4x12-3

Kit
10-3x
11-4

Dining
13-1x13-2

R

W

W
D
F

Great Rm
13-1x10-3

L

Br 2
11-7x10-0

Br 3
11-1x10-0

Porch

 **CUSTOMIZER KiT** Customize This Plan **SEE PAGE 4**

 **MATERIAL LIST $** Material List Available **SEE PAGE 81**

Large Living And Dining Area

> 1,160 total square feet of living area

Special features

- U-shaped kitchen includes breakfast bar and convenient laundry area
- Master bedroom features private half bath and large closet
- Dining room with handy outdoor access
- Dining room and great room combine to create open living atmosphere
- 3 bedrooms, 1 1/2 baths
- Crawl space foundation, drawings also include basement and slab foundations

Price Code AA

Plan #556-0543

To order blueprints use the form on page 83 or call 1-800-DREAM HOME (373-2646)

BELCOURT

Spacious Master Suite Adds Luxury

1,596 total square feet of living area

Special features

- Large corner fireplace enhances living area
- Centrally located utility room provides convenient access
- Master bath features double walk-in closets, oversized tub and plant shelves
- Both the living area and master suite are accented with raised ceilings
- Bay window in dining area adds interest and light
- 3 bedrooms, 2 baths
- Slab foundation

Price Code B

CUSTOMIZER KIT
Customize This Plan
SEE PAGE 4

MATERIAL LIST $$
Material List Available
SEE PAGE 81

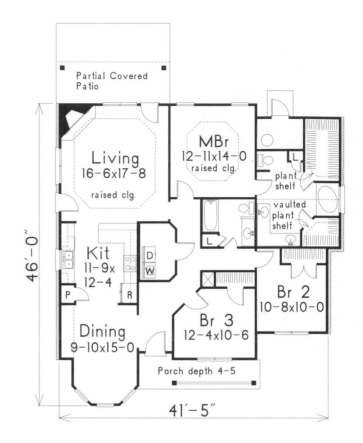

Plan #556-0687

Plan #556-1129-A-1 basement
Plan #556-1129-A-2 crawl space & slab

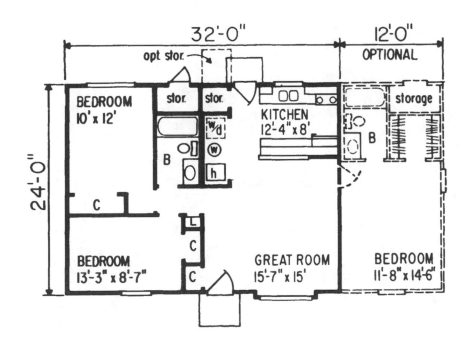

Functional Livability In A Small Ranch

> 768 total square feet of living area

Special features

- Great room has an attractive box window for enjoying views
- Kitchen has large window and is open to dining area
- Six closets provide great storage for a compact plan
- Plans include optional third bedroom with 288 square feet
- 2 bedrooms, 1 bath
- Basement foundation or crawl space and slab foundation drawings available, please specify when ordering

Price Code AAA

Material List Available
SEE PAGE 81

CONCORD

Spacious Vaulted Great Room

 Customize This Plan **SEE PAGE 4**

 Material List Available **SEE PAGE 81**

| 1,189 total square feet of living area |

Special features

- All bedrooms are located on the second floor
- Dining room and kitchen both have views of the patio
- Convenient half bath located near the kitchen
- Master bedroom has private bath
- 3 bedrooms, 2 1/2 baths, 2-car garage
- Basement foundation
- 615 square feet on the first floor and 574 square feet on the second floor

Price Code AA

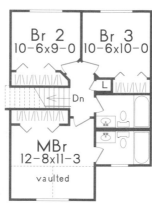

Second Floor

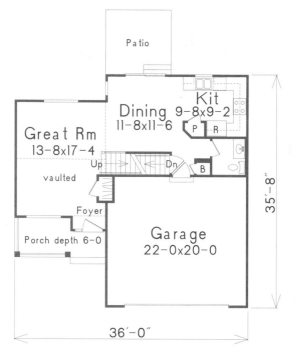

First Floor

Plan #556-0487

ROCKWOOD

Sculptured Roof Line And Facade Add Charm

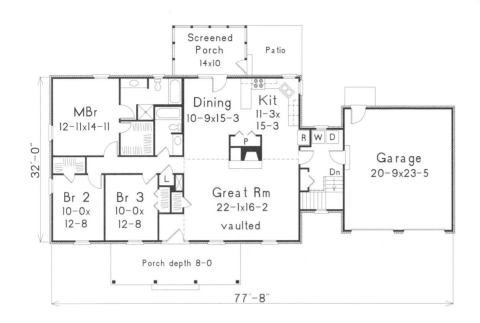

Screened Porch 14x10

Patio

MBr 12-11x14-11

Dining 10-9x15-3

Kit 11-3x 15-3

 P

R W D

Garage 20-9x23-5

Dn

32'-0"

Br 2 10-0x 12-8

Br 3 10-0x 12-8

 L

Great Rm 22-1x16-2

vaulted

Porch depth 8-0

77'-8"

1,674 total square feet of living area

Special features

- Great room, dining area and kitchen, surrounded with vaulted ceiling, central fireplace and log bin

- Convenient laundry/mud room located between garage and family area with handy stairs to basement

- Easily expandable screened porch and adjacent patio with access from dining area

- Master bedroom features full bath with tub, separate shower and walk-in closet

- 3 bedrooms, 2 baths, 2-car garage

- Basement foundation, drawings also include crawl space and slab foundations

Price Code B

CUSTOMIZER KIT Customize This Plan **SEE PAGE 4**

MATERIAL LIST $ Material List Available **SEE PAGE 81**

Plan #556-0227

WEDGEWOOD

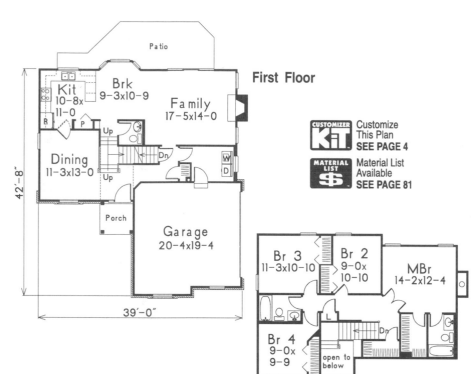

First Floor

Kit 10-8x11-0
Brk 9-3x10-9
Family 17-5x14-0
Dining 11-3x13-0
Patio
Porch
Garage 20-4x19-4
42'-8"
39'-0"

CUSTOMIZER KiT Customize This Plan SEE PAGE 4

MATERIAL LIST $ Material List Available SEE PAGE 81

Second Floor

Br 3 11-3x10-10
Br 2 9-0x10-10
MBr 14-2x12-4
Br 4 9-0x9-9
open to below

Smaller Home Offers Stylish Exterior

1,700 total square feet of living area

Special features

- Two-story entry with T-stair is illuminated with decorative oval window
- Skillfully designed U-shaped kitchen with built-in pantry
- All bedrooms have generous closet storage and are common to spacious hall with walk-in cedar closet
- 4 bedrooms, 2 1/2 baths, 2-car garage
- Basement foundation
- 896 square feet on the first floor and 804 square feet on the second floor

Price Code B

Plan #556-0656

BROADMOOR

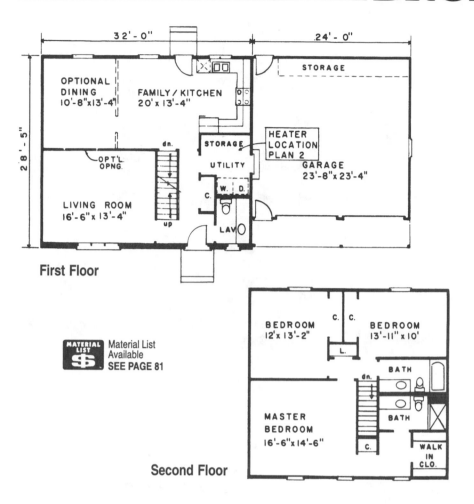

First Floor

MATERIAL LIST $ Material List Available SEE PAGE 81

Second Floor

Traditional Family Two-Story

1,837 total square feet of living area

Special features

- Master suite expands entire front of second floor including private bath and walk-in closet

- Spacious family/kitchen area with option for an enclosed dining comprises most of the first floor

- Utility room has access to garage and maintains plenty of extra space for storage

- 3 bedrooms, 2 1/2 baths, 2-car garage

- Basement foundation or crawl space and slab foundation drawings available, please specify when ordering

- 909 square feet on the first floor and 928 square feet on the second floor

Price Code C

Plan #556-ES-102-1 basement
Plan #556-ES-102-2 crawl space & slab

SPRINGFIELD

Charming Home Arranged For Open Living

1,609 total square feet of living area

Special features

- Kitchen captures full use of space with pantry, ample cabinets and workspace
- Master bedroom well secluded with walk-in closet and private bath
- Large utility room includes sink and extra storage
- Attractive bay window in dining area provides light
- 3 bedrooms, 2 1/2 baths, 2-car garage
- Slab foundation
- 1,072 square feet on the first floor and 537 square feet on the second floor

Price Code B

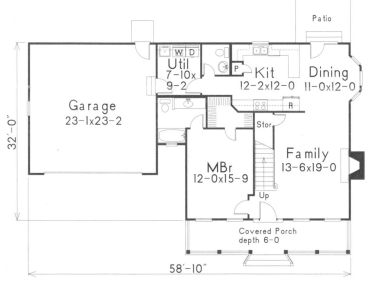

First Floor

First floor labels: Patio; W D; Util 7-10x9-2; P; Kit 12-2x12-0; Dining 11-0x12-0; Garage 23-1x23-2; R; Stor; Family 13-6x19-0; MBr 12-0x15-9; Up; 32'-0"; 58'-10"; Covered Porch depth 6-0

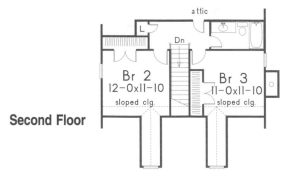

Second Floor

Second floor labels: attic; L; Dn; Br 2 12-0x11-10 sloped clg.; Br 3 11-0x11-10 sloped clg.

Customize This Plan **SEE PAGE 4**

Material List Available **SEE PAGE 81**

Plan #556-0686

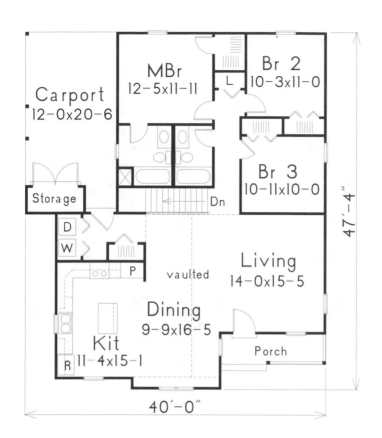

Compact Home With Functional Design

1,396 total square feet of living area

Special features

- Gabled front adds interest to facade
- Living and dining rooms share a vaulted ceiling
- Master bedroom features a walk-in closet and private bath
- Functional kitchen with a center work island and convenient pantry
- 3 bedrooms, 2 baths, 1-car carport
- Basement foundation, drawings also include crawl space foundation

Price Code A

CUSTOMIZER KiT — Customize This Plan SEE PAGE 4

MATERIAL LIST $ — Material List Available SEE PAGE 81

Plan #556-0296

OAKBRIAR

Vaulted Ceilings Highlight This Home

1,560 total square feet of living area

Special features

- Cozy breakfast room is tucked at the rear of this home and features plenty of windows for natural light
- Large entry has easy access to secondary bedrooms, laundry/utility, dining and living rooms
- Private master suite
- Kitchen overlooks living room with fireplace and patio access
- 3 bedrooms, 2 baths, 2-car garage
- Slab foundation

Price Code B

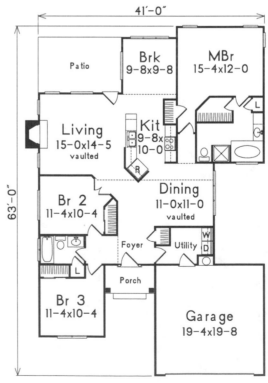

41'-0"

63'-0"

Patio

Brk
9-8x9-8

MBr
15-4x12-0

Living
15-0x14-5
vaulted

Kit
9-8x
10-0

Br 2
11-4x10-4

Dining
11-0x11-0
vaulted

Foyer

Utility

W
D

Br 3
11-4x10-4

Porch

Garage
19-4x19-8

CUSTOMIZER KiT — Customize This Plan SEE PAGE 4

MATERIAL LIST $ — Material List Available SEE PAGE 81

Plan #556-0667

PROVIDER II

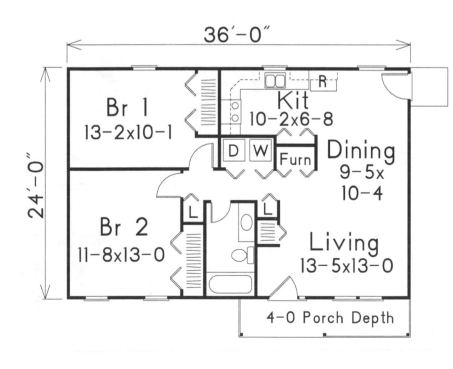

36´-0"

24´-0"

Br 1
13-2x10-1

Kit
10-2x6-8

R

D W Furn

Dining
9-5x
10-4

Br 2
11-8x13-0

L L

Living
13-5x13-0

4-0 Porch Depth

Perfect Home For A Small Family

864 total square feet of living area

Special features

- L-shaped kitchen with convenient pantry is adjacent to dining area
- Easy access to laundry area, linen closet and storage closet
- Both bedrooms include ample closet space
- 2 bedrooms, 1 bath
- Crawl space foundation, drawings also include basement and slab foundations

Price Code AAA

Customize This Plan
SEE PAGE 4

Material List Available
SEE PAGE 81

Plan #556-0502

TREEBROOKE

Country Kitchen Center Of Living Activities

1,556 total square feet of living area

Special features

- A compact home with all the amenities
- Country kitchen combines practicality with access to other areas for eating and entertaining
- Two-way fireplace joins the dining and living areas
- Plant shelf and vaulted ceiling highlight the master bedroom
- 3 bedrooms, 2 1/2 baths, 2-car garage
- Basement foundation
- 834 square feet on the first floor and 722 square feet on the second floor

Price Code B

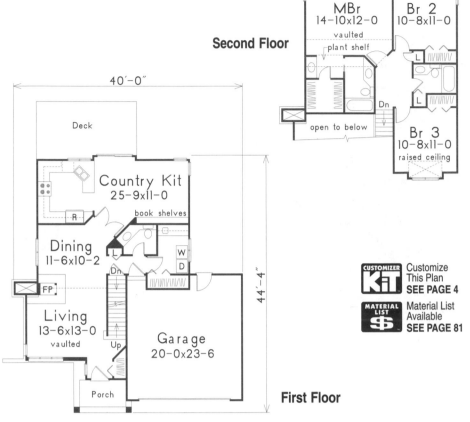

Second Floor

MBr 14-10x12-0 vaulted
plant shelf
Br 2 10-8x11-0
Br 3 10-8x11-0 raised ceiling
open to below

40'-0"
Deck
Country Kit 25-9x11-0
book shelves
Dining 11-6x10-2
Living 13-6x13-0 vaulted
Garage 20-0x23-6
Porch
FP
44'-4"

First Floor

CUSTOMIZER KiT Customize This Plan **SEE PAGE 4**

MATERIAL LIST $ Material List Available **SEE PAGE 81**

Plan #556-0209

RUTHERFORD

Plan #556-T-109-1 basement
Plan #556-T-109-2 crawl space & slab

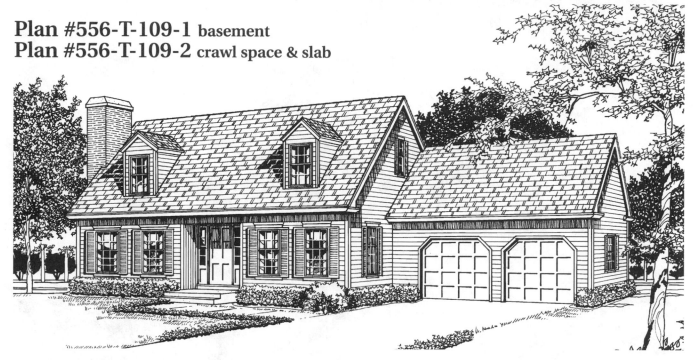

Design Has Traditional Elegance

1,872 total square feet of living area

Special features

- Recessed porch has entry door with sidelights and roof dormers adding charm

- Foyer with handcrafted stair adjoins living room with fireplace

- First floor bedroom with access to bath and laundry room is perfect for master suite or live-in parent

- Largest of three second floor bedrooms enjoys his and hers closets and private access to hall bath

- 4 bedrooms, 2 baths, 2-car garage

- Basement foundation or crawl space and slab foundation drawings available, please specify when ordering

- 1,068 square feet on the first floor and 804 square feet on the second floor

Price Code C

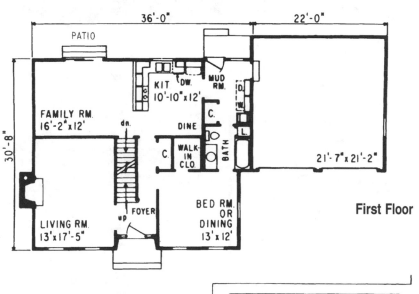

PATIO

36'-0"   22'-0"

KIT 10'-10"x12'   MUD RM.

FAMILY RM. 16'-2"x12'   DINE

LIVING RM. 13'x17'-5"   FOYER   WALK-IN CLO.   BATH

dn.   up

BED RM. OR DINING 13'x12'

21'-7"x21'-2"

30'-8"

First Floor

MATERIAL LIST $ Material List Available **SEE PAGE 81**

Second Floor

C.   DRESS. AREA   BATH

BED RM. 11'-6"x11'-6"

BED RM. 13'x15'   dn   BED RM. 14'x11'

STOR.

LEXBURG

Open Layout Ensures Easy Living

976 total square feet of living area

Special features

- Cozy front porch opens into large living room
- Convenient half bath is located on first floor
- All bedrooms are located upstairs for privacy
- Dining room has access to the outdoors
- 3 bedrooms, 1 1/2 baths
- Basement foundation
- 488 square feet on the first floor and 488 square feet on the second floor

Price Code AA

CUSTOMIZER KiT — Customize This Plan **SEE PAGE 4**

MATERIAL LIST $S — Material List Available **SEE PAGE 81**

Kit
10-0x7-10

Dining
11-5x8-0

Living
11-5x17-6

Dn

Up

Porch Depth
4-0

26'-0"

20'-0"

First Floor

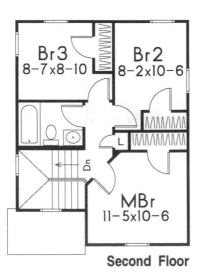

Br3
8-7x8-10

Br2
8-2x10-6

Dn

MBr
11-5x10-6

Second Floor

Plan #556-0493

WINTERGREEN

Tall Windows, Sweeping Roof Lines Make A Sizable Impression

1,351 total square feet of living area

Special features

- Roof lines and vaulted ceilings make this home look larger than its true size
- Central fireplace provides a focal point for dining and living areas
- Master bedroom suite is highlighted by a roomy window seat and a walk-in closet
- 3 bedrooms, 2 1/2 baths, 2-car garage
- Basement foundation
- 674 square feet on the first floor and 677 square feet on the second floor

Price Code A

Second Floor

MBr
11-8x14-0
vaulted

Loft
9-0x
12-6

Br 2
10-0x
14-0

Dn

open to below

48'-0"

First Floor

29'-10"

Deck

Garage
19-8x23-4

Kit

Dining
11-0x13-4

Living
18-0x12-8
vaulted

10-4x11-0

Dn

Up

Customize
This Plan
SEE PAGE 4

Material List
Available
SEE PAGE 81

Plan #556-0103

SUNWOOD

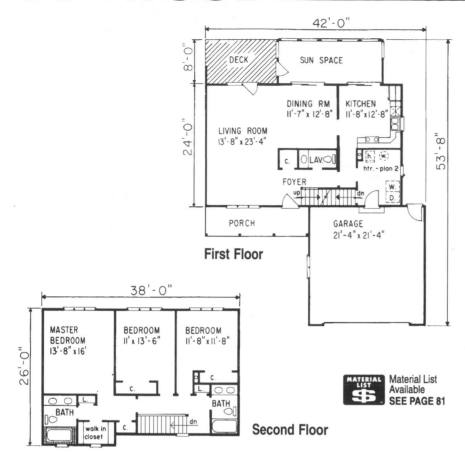

First Floor

- 42'-0"
- 8'-0"
- 24'-0"
- 53'-8"

DECK

SUN SPACE

DINING RM
11'-7" x 12'-8"

KITCHEN
11'-8" x 12'-8"

LIVING ROOM
13'-8" x 23'-4"

c.   LAV.

h   w
htr. - plan 2

FOYER
up   dn

W.
D.

PORCH

GARAGE
21'-4" x 21'-4"

Second Floor

- 38'-0"
- 26'-0"

MASTER
BEDROOM
13'-8" x 16'

BEDROOM
11' x 13'-6"

BEDROOM
11'-8" x 11'-8"

c.

c.

L

L

c.

BATH

BATH

walk in
closet

c.   dn

MATERIAL LIST $ Material List Available **SEE PAGE 81**

Capture The Sun

| 1,852 total square feet of living area |

Special features

- Exterior appearance is heightened with use of covered porch, decorative octagonal window and cupola
- Grand-sized living room presents itself upon entering and relishes in front and rear views
- The dining and kitchen access a beautiful sunroom immersed in light from surrounding windows
- 3 bedrooms, 2 1/2 baths, 2-car garage
- Basement foundation or crawl space and slab foundation drawings available, please specify when ordering
- 912 square feet on the first floor and 940 square feet on the second floor

Price Code C

Plan #556-1214-1 basement
Plan #556-1214-2 crawl space & slab

CROSSWOOD

Ideal For Starter Home

800 total square feet of living area

Special features

- Master bedroom with walk-in closet and private access to bath
- Large living room features handy coat closet
- Kitchen includes side entrance, closet and convenient laundry area
- 2 bedrooms, 1 bath
- Crawl space foundation, drawings also include basement and slab foundations

Price Code AAA

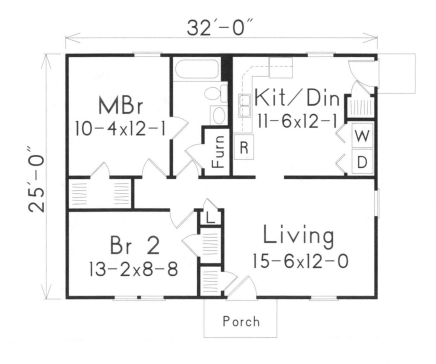

32'-0"

25'-0"

MBr
10-4x12-1

Kit/Din
11-6x12-1

Furn

R

W
D

Br 2
13-2x8-8

Living
15-6x12-0

L

Porch

 Customize This Plan SEE PAGE 4

 Material List Available SEE PAGE 81

Plan #556-0582

ROCKVALE

Compact Ranch With Covered Porch

1,264 total square feet of living area

Special features

- Master bedroom with private bath
- Kitchen nestled between family room and living room for convenience
- Third bedroom entry has double-doors and would make a perfect office or library
- Large storage area inside garage
- 3 bedrooms, 2 baths, 2-car garage
- Basement foundation or crawl space and slab foundation drawings available, please specify when ordering

Price Code A

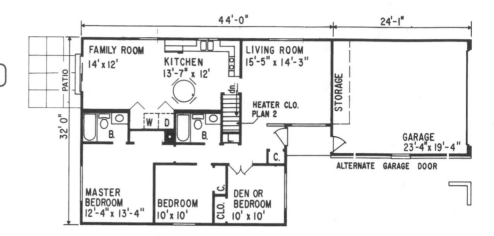

Material List Available
SEE PAGE 81

Plan #556-N288-1 basement
Plan #556-N288-2 crawl space & slab

SABRINA

Pillared Front Porch Generates Charm And Warmth

1,567 total square feet of living area

Special features

- Living room flows into dining room shaped by an angled pass-through into the kitchen
- Cheerful, windowed dinette
- Upstairs has 338 square feet for future space and is well-lit from four dormers
- Bedrooms flank both sides of the living room, master suite located for privacy, two identical bedrooms on other side share a bath
- 3 bedrooms, 2 baths, 2-car side entry garage
- Basement foundation, drawings also include slab foundation

Price Code B

First Floor

67'-6"

46'-8"

Garage 21-0x20-0

Storage

Terrace

Brk 8-10x 6-8

Kit 11-0x 12-0

W D

R

Dining 11-0x12-0

Br 2 12-2x10-0

L

MBr 16-2x13-6

Dn

Up

Living 15-0x19-0

Br 3 12-2x10-0

Porch depth 6-6

Second Floor

Dn Future Area 22-4x15-0

CUSTOMIZER KiT Customize This Plan **SEE PAGE 4**

MATERIAL LIST $ Material List Available **SEE PAGE 81**

Plan #556-0678

BROOKDALE

Formal And Informal Gathering Rooms

1,314 total square feet of living area

Special features

- U-shaped kitchen joins cozy dining area
- Family room has outside access
- Roomy closets serve the second floor bedrooms
- 3 bedrooms, 1 1/2 baths, 2-car garage
- Basement foundation, drawings also include crawl space foundation
- 762 square feet on the first floor and 552 square feet on the second floor

Price Code A

CUSTOMIZER KIT Customize This Plan **SEE PAGE 4**

MATERIAL LIST $ Material List Available **SEE PAGE 81**

Second Floor

Br 2
13-1x10-1

Dn
L

MBr
11-2x12-7

Br 3
9-10x9-3

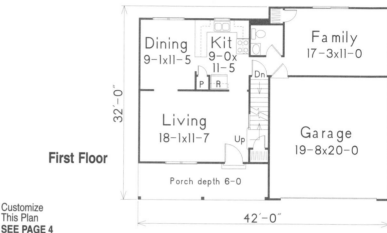

First Floor

Dining
9-1x11-5

Kit
9-0x
11-5

Family
17-3x11-0

P R
Dn

Living
18-1x11-7

Up

Garage
19-8x20-0

32'-0"

Porch depth 6-0

42'-0"

Plan #556-0196

BURLINGTON I

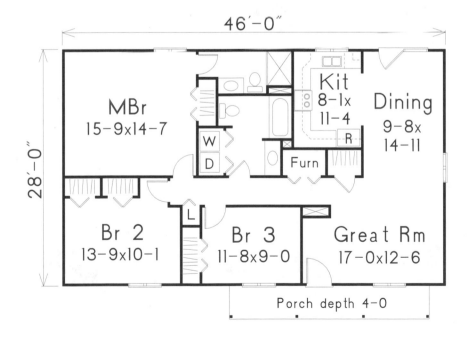

46'-0"

28'-0"

MBr
15-9x14-7

W
D

Kit
8-1x
11-4

Dining
9-8x
14-11

Furn

R

Br 2
13-9x10-1

L

Br 3
11-8x9-0

Great Rm
17-0x12-6

Porch depth 4-0

 Customize
This Plan
SEE PAGE 4

 Material List
Available
SEE PAGE 81

Peaceful Shaded Front Porch

1,288 total square feet of living area

Special features

■ Kitchen, dining, and great rooms join to create open living space

■ Master bedroom includes private bath

■ Secondary bedrooms include ample closet space

■ Hall bath features convenient laundry closet

■ Dining room accesses outdoors

■ 3 bedrooms, 2 baths

■ Crawl space foundation, drawings also include basement and slab foundations

Price Code A

Plan #556-0534

RIDGELAND

Efficient Layout In This Multi-Level Home

1,617 total square feet of living area

Special features

- Kitchen/breakfast area overlooks great room with fireplace
- Formal dining room features vaulted ceiling and elegant circle-top window
- For privacy, all bedrooms are located on the same level
- 3 bedrooms, 2 1/2 baths, 2-car garage
- Partial crawl space/slab foundation
- 876 square feet on the first floor and 741 square feet on the second floor

Price Code B

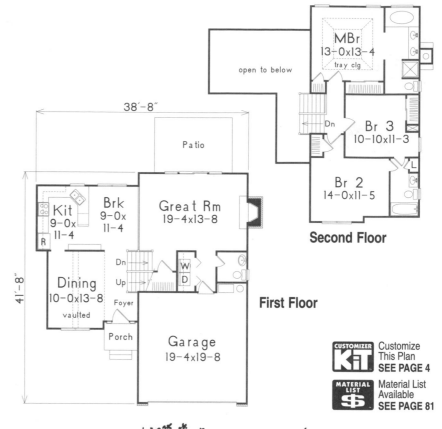

Second Floor

MBr 13-0x13-4 tray clg
open to below
Br 3 10-10x11-3
Br 2 14-0x11-5

38'-8"

41'-8"

Patio
Kit 9-0x11-4
Brk 9-0x11-4
Great Rm 19-4x13-8
Dining 10-0x13-8 vaulted
Dn
Up
W D
Foyer
Porch
Garage 19-4x19-8

First Floor

CUSTOMIZER KIT — Customize This Plan SEE PAGE 4

MATERIAL LIST — Material List Available SEE PAGE 81

Plan #556-0668

TIMBERLAND

Compact Ranch An Ideal Starter Home

988 total square feet of living area

Special features

- Great room features corner fireplace
- Vaulted ceiling and corner windows add space and light in great room
- Eat-in kitchen with vaulted ceiling accesses deck for outdoor living
- Master bedroom features separate vanity and private access to the bathroom
- 2 bedrooms, 1 bath, 2-car garage
- Basement foundation

Price Code AA

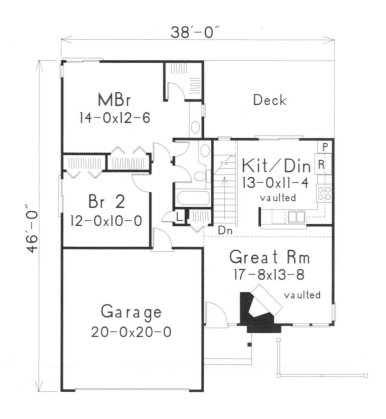

Plan #556-0273

WESTERRY

Answer To A Tapered Lot

986 total square feet of living area

Special features

- Wide and tall windows in living and dining/kitchen areas provide bright and cheery spaces for your enjoyment

- Three bedrooms with plenty of closet space and oversized hall bath are located in rear wing of home

- An extra deep garage has storage space at rear and access to patio behind garage

- Convenient linen closet located in hall

- 3 bedrooms, 1 bath, 1-car garage

- Basement foundation, drawings also include crawl space and slab foundations

    Price Code AA

Material List Available
SEE PAGE 81

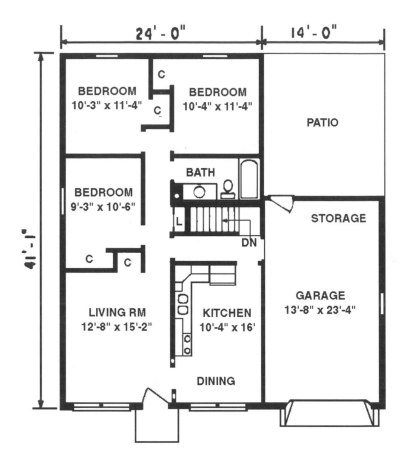

Plan #556-S-114

Home For Narrow Lot Offers Wide Open Spaces

1,492 total square feet of living area

Special features

- Cleverly angled entry spills into living and dining rooms which share warmth of fireplace flanked by arched windows

- Master suite includes double-door entry, huge walk-in closet, shower and bath with picture window

- Stucco and dutch hipped roofs add warmth and charm to facade

- 3 bedrooms, 2 1/2 baths, 2-car garage

- Basement foundation

- 760 square feet on the first floor and 732 square feet on the second floor

    Price Code A

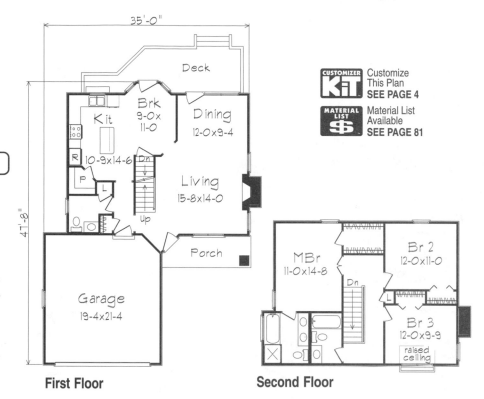

Customize This Plan **SEE PAGE 4**

Material List Available **SEE PAGE 81**

First Floor

Second Floor

J.N. HANSEN S.D.G.

Plan #556-0415

WISTAR

Corner Windows Brighten Charming 1 1/2 Story

1,703 total square feet of living area

Special features

- Large fireplace, French doors onto patio and plant shelves in living room
- Protected front entry with raised ceiling in foyer
- Master bedroom with walk-in closet, vaulted ceiling and window seats
- Well-suited for a narrow lot
- 3 bedrooms, 2 1/2 baths, 2-car garage
- Slab foundation, drawings also include crawl space foundation
- 1,163 square feet on the first floor and 540 square feet on the second floor

Price Code B

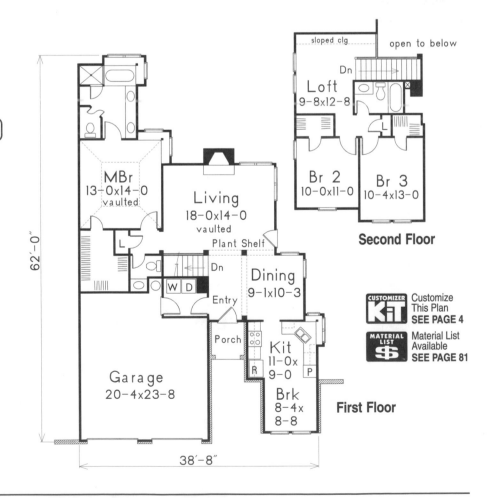

Second Floor

First Floor

CUSTOMIZER KiT — Customize This Plan SEE PAGE 4

MATERIAL LIST $$ — Material List Available SEE PAGE 81

Plan #556-0115

Convenient Ranch

1,120 total square feet of living area

Special features

- Master bedroom includes a half bath with laundry area, linen closet and kitchen access

- Kitchen has charming double door entry, breakfast bar and a convenient walk-in pantry

- Welcoming front porch opens to large living room with coat closet

- 3 bedrooms, 1 1/2 baths

- Crawl space foundation, drawings also include basement and slab foundations

Price Code AA

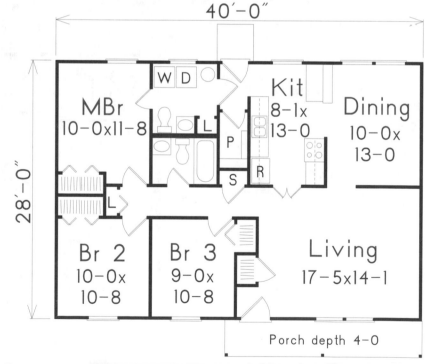

40'-0"

28'-0"

MBr
10-0x11-8

Kit
8-1x
13-0

Dining
10-0x
13-0

W D

P

L

S

R

Br 2
10-0x
10-8

Br 3
9-0x
10-8

Living
17-5x14-1

Porch depth 4-0

Customize This Plan
SEE PAGE 4

Material List Available
SEE PAGE 81

Plan #556-0587

AVA

Rustic
Stone Exterior

CUSTOMIZER **KiT** — Customize This Plan **SEE PAGE 4**

MATERIAL LIST $ — Material List Available **SEE PAGE 81**

1,466 total square feet of living area

Special features

- Energy efficient home with 2" x 6" exterior walls
- Foyer separates the living room from the dining room and contains a generous coat closet
- Large living room with corner fireplace, bay window and pass-through to the kitchen
- Informal breakfast room opens out to large terrace through a sliding glass door which lets light into area
- Master bedroom has a large walk-in closet and private bath
- 3 bedrooms, 2 baths, 2-car garage
- Basement foundation, drawings also include slab foundation

Price Code A

56'-4"

49'-8"

Br 3
10-4x
10-0

MBr
14-10x14-4

Br 2
13-4x10-0

Kit
11-0x9-0

Brk
8-8x
9-0

Porch

Living
14-10x14-4

Dining
10-0x11-0

Dn

D
W

Garage
20-0x19-6

shelf

Porch depth 6-0

Plan #556-0679

Innovative Ranch Has Cozy Corner Patio

1,092 total square feet of living area

Special features

- Box window and inviting porch with dormers creates a charming facade

- Eat-in kitchen offers a pass-through breakfast bar, corner window wall to patio, pantry and convenient laundry with half bath

- Master bedroom features double entry doors and walk-in closet

- 3 bedrooms, 1 1/2 baths, 1-car garage

- Basement foundation

    Price Code AA

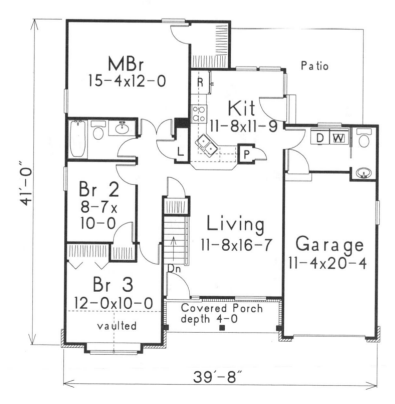

Plan #556-0478

CRESTLAND

Well-Planned Split-Level Family Living

1,004 total square feet of living area

Special features

- Oversized country kitchen includes room for dining area and lots of cabinetry
- Sleeping area separate from rest of home for privacy
- Lower level includes optional large utility room and half bath or keep family room space spacious and open
- 3 bedrooms, 1 bath, optional 2-car garage
- Partial basement/crawl space foundation

Price Code AA

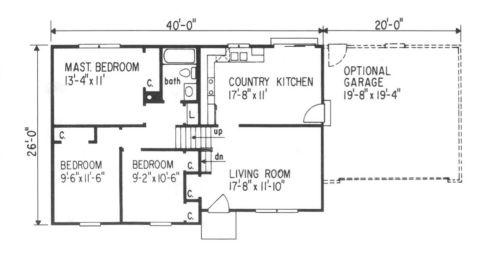

40'-0"   20'-0"

MAST. BEDROOM
13'-4" x 11'

bath

COUNTRY KITCHEN
17'-8" x 11'

OPTIONAL
GARAGE
19'-8" x 19'-4"

c.

26'-0"

c.

up

dn

BEDROOM
9'-6" x 11'-6"

BEDROOM
9'-2" x 10'-6"

c.

c.

LIVING ROOM
17'-8" x 11'-10"

c.

Material List Available
SEE PAGE 81

Plan #556-ES-152

DUNWOOD

Compact Home For Functional Living

1,220 total square feet of living area

Special features

- Vaulted ceilings add luxury to living room and master suite
- Spacious living room accented with a large fireplace and hearth
- Gracious dining area is adjacent to the convenient wrap-around kitchen
- Washer and dryer handy to the bedrooms
- Covered porch entry adds appeal
- Rear sundeck adjoins dining area
- 3 bedrooms, 2 baths, 2-car drive under garage
- Basement foundation

Price Code A

CUSTOMIZER KIT Customize This Plan SEE PAGE 4

MATERIAL LIST $ Material List Available SEE PAGE 81

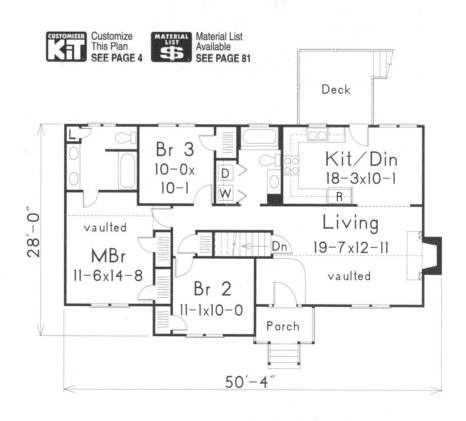

Deck

Br 3
10-0x
10-1

Kit/Din
18-3x10-1

vaulted

MBr
11-6x14-8

Br 2
11-1x10-0

Living
19-7x12-11

vaulted

Porch

28'-0"

50'-4"

Plan #556-0173

WILSON

Spacious And Centrally Located Family Area

> 1,539 total square feet of living area

Special features

- Large master suite with private bath has access to patio
- Convenient laundry room located between carport and kitchen
- Bedrooms secluded off living areas for added privacy
- Private dining area with bay window for elegant entertaining
- Attached carport offers additional roomy storage area
- 3 bedrooms, 2 baths, 2-car attached carport
- Slab foundation

Price Code B

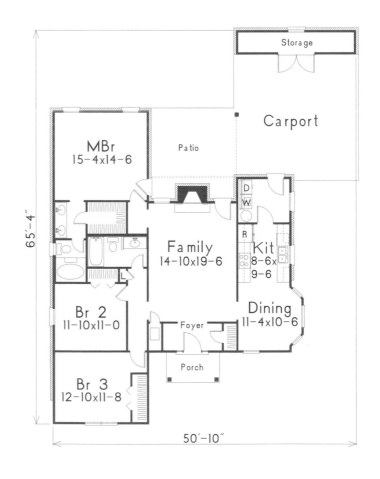

 Customize This Plan
SEE PAGE 4

 Material List Available
SEE PAGE 81

Plan #556-0689

FOXCREEK

Desirable Design For Narrow Site

1,082 total square feet of living area

Special features

- A convenient coat closet is located just inside entryway
- Large living room offers optional double-doors into a den
- Extremely functional kitchen leads to dining room with sliding glass doors opening onto rear patio
- Nice-sized bedrooms enjoy plenty of large closet space
- 3 bedrooms, 1 bath, 2-car garage
- Basement foundation or crawl space foundation drawings available, please specify when ordering

Price Code AA

Plan #556-N293-1 basement
Plan #556-N293-2 crawl space

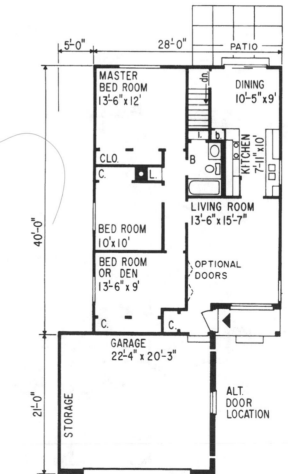

Material List Available
SEE PAGE 81

SHELBURNE

Plan #556-1197-1 basement
Plan #556-1197-2 crawl space & slab

Energy Efficient Home

1,536 total square feet of living area

Special features

- Formal living room area featured in the front of the home
- Combined living areas create the back of the home with great room, dining and kitchen all in one
- Second floor master bedroom includes private bath
- 3 bedrooms, 2 1/2 baths, 1-car garage
- Basement foundation or crawl space and slab foundation drawings available, please specify when ordering
- 768 square feet on the first floor and 768 square feet on the second floor

Price Code B

MATERIAL LIST $ Material List Available **SEE PAGE 81**

Second Floor

BED RM. 11'-6"x11'
BED RM. 11'-3"x10'
C.
C.
C. C.
dn.
flue- plan 2
BATH
MASTER BEDRM. 11'-6"x15'
BATH

First Floor

24'-0"
DINE.
opt. fireplace
GREAT RM. 23'-3" x 12'-10"
bar
32'-0"
LIVING RM. 11'-6" x 15'
dn.
up
ONE CAR 13'-8"
TWO CAR 21'-8"
GARAGE 13'-4"x21'-4"
LAV
storage
FOYER
C.
4'-0"

CYPRESS

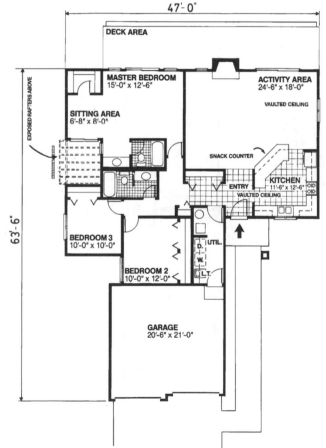

47'- 0"

DECK AREA

EXPOSED RAFTERS ABOVE

63'- 6"

MASTER BEDROOM
15'-0" x 12'-6"

SITTING AREA
6'-8" x 8'-0"

ACTIVITY AREA
24'-6" x 18'-0"

VAULTED CEILING

SNACK COUNTER

ENTRY

KITCHEN
11'-6" x 12'-6"

VAULTED CEILING

BEDROOM 3
10'-0" x 10'-0"

D.
W.

L.T.

UTIL.

BEDROOM 2
10'-0" x 12'-0"

GARAGE
20'-6" x 21'-0"

Multiple Gabled Roofs Add Drama

1,533 total square feet of living area

Special features

- Private deck outside the master bedroom sitting area

- Sloped ceilings add volume to the large activity area

- Activity room has fireplace, snack bar and shares access to the backyard with the master bedroom

- Convenient utility room located near the garage

- 3 bedrooms, 2 bath, 2-car garage

- Basement/crawl space foundation or slab foundation drawings available, please specify when ordering

  Price Code B

Plan #556-1276-1 partial basement/crawl space
Plan #556-1276-2 slab

 Material List Available
SEE PAGE 81

FOXBRIAR

Compact, Convenient And Charming

> 1,266 total square feet of living area

Special features

- Narrow frontage is perfect for small lots

- Energy efficient home with 2" x 6" exterior walls

- Prominent central hall provides a convenient connection for all main rooms

- Design incorporates full-size master bedroom complete with dressing room, bath and walk-in closet

- Angled kitchen includes handy laundry facilities and is adjacent to an oversized storage area

- 3 bedrooms, 2 baths, 2-car rear entry garage

- Crawl space foundation, drawings also include slab foundation

    Price Code A

CUSTOMIZER KiT Customize This Plan **SEE PAGE 4**

MATERIAL LIST $ Material List Available **SEE PAGE 81**

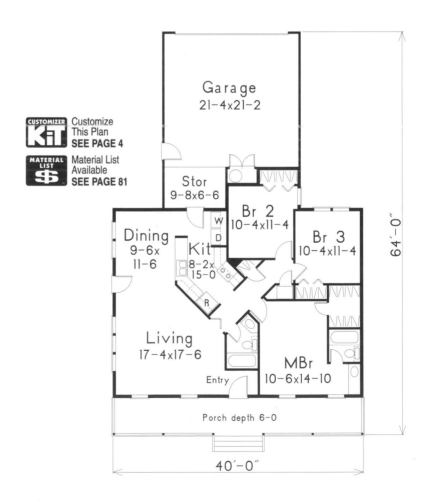

Plan #556-0192

TIMBERHILL

Energy Efficient Design With Plenty Of Extras

1,064 total square feet of living area

Special features

- Well-designed country kitchen
- Living room and kitchen unite to provide central living area
- Lots of closet space throughout perfect for ski storage or other sporting gear
- Unique built-in planter adds appeal to the front exterior
- 3 bedrooms, 1 1/2 baths, 2-car garage
- Basement or crawl space and slab foundation drawings available, please specify when ordering

Price Code AA

Material List Available
SEE PAGE 81

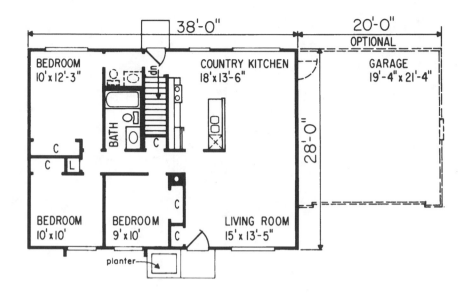

Plan #556-1131-B-1 basement
Plan #556-1131-B-2 crawl space & slab

NORWICK

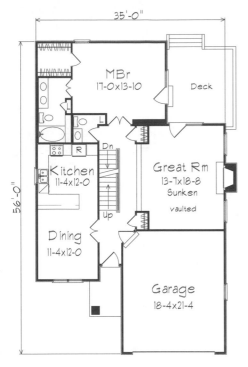

35'-0"

56'-0"

MBr
17-0x13-10

Deck

Kitchen
11-4x12-0

Dn

R

Up

Great Rm
13-7x18-8
Sunken
vaulted

Dining
11-4x12-0

Garage
18-4x21-4

First Floor

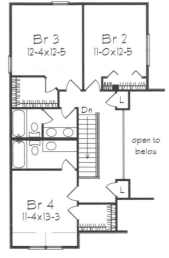

Br 3
12-4x12-5

Br 2
11-0x12-5

Dn

open to below

Br 4
11-4x13-3

Second Floor

Great Room's Symmetry Steals The Show

> 1,985 total square feet of living area

Special features

- Charming design for narrow lot
- Dramatic sunken great room features vaulted ceiling, large double-hung windows and transomed patio doors
- Grand master suite includes double entry doors, large closet, elegant bath and patio access
- 4 bedrooms, 3 1/2 baths, 2-car garage
- Basement foundation
- 1,114 square feet on the first floor and 871 square feet on the second floor

Price Code C

CUSTOMIZER KiT Customize This Plan **SEE PAGE 4**

MATERIAL LIST $ Material List Available **SEE PAGE 81**

Plan #556-0416

GRASS ROOTS I

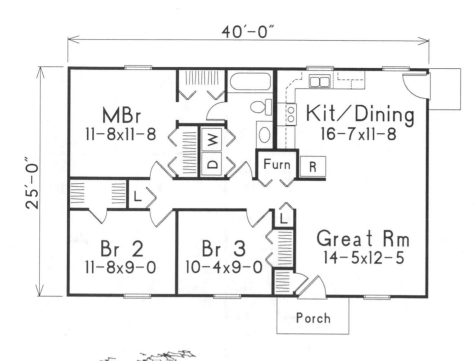

40'-0"

25'-0"

MBr
11-8x11-8

Kit/Dining
16-7x11-8

D W

L

Furn
R

Br 2
11-8x9-0

Br 3
10-4x9-0

L

Great Rm
14-5x12-5

Porch

Open Living Space Creates Comfortable Atmosphere

1,000 total square feet of living area

Special features

- Bath includes convenient closeted laundry area
- Master bedroom includes double closets and private access to bath
- Foyer features handy coat closet
- L-shaped kitchen provides easy outside access
- 3 bedrooms, 1 bath
- Crawl space foundation, drawings also include basement and slab foundations

Price Code AA

CUSTOMIZER KiT Customize This Plan **SEE PAGE 4**

MATERIAL LIST $ Material List Available **SEE PAGE 81**

Plan #556-0503

To order blueprints use the form on page 83 or call 1-800-DREAM HOME (373-2646)

WESTOVER

Compact Home, Perfect Fit For Narrow Lot

1,085 total square feet of living area

Special features

- Rear porch has a handy access through the kitchen
- Convenient hall linen closet located on the second floor
- Breakfast bar in kitchen offers additional counter space
- Living and dining rooms combine for open living atmosphere
- 3 bedrooms, 2 baths
- Basement foundation
- 685 square feet on the first floor and 400 square feet on the second floor

Price Code AA

 Customize This Plan **SEE PAGE 4** Material List Available **SEE PAGE 81**

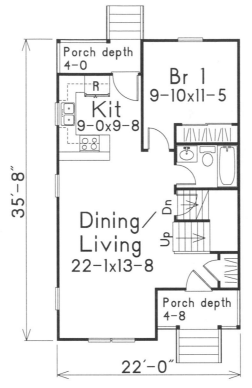

Porch depth 4-0

R

Kit 9-0x9-8

Br 1 9-10x11-5

Dining/ Living 22-1x13-8

Up Dn

Porch depth 4-8

35'-8"

22'-0"

First Floor

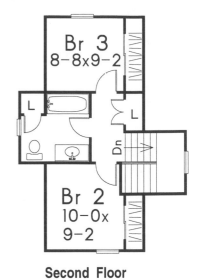

Br 3 8-8x9-2

L

L

Dn

Br 2 10-0x 9-2

Second Floor

Plan #556-0494

FERNWOOD

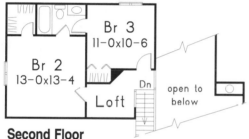

Second Floor

Br 2
13-0x13-4

Br 3
11-0x10-6

Loft

Dn

open to
below

Vaulted Living Area With Corner Fireplace

[1,448 total square feet of living area]

Special features

- Dining room conveniently adjoins kitchen and accesses rear deck
- Private first floor master bedroom
- Secondary bedrooms share a bath and cozy loft area
- 3 bedrooms, 2 1/2 baths, 2-car garage
- Basement foundation
- 972 square feet on the first floor and 476 square feet on the second floor

Price Code A

CUSTOMIZER KIT Customize This Plan **SEE PAGE 4**

MATERIAL LIST $ Material List Available **SEE PAGE 81**

40'-0"

40'-0"

Deck

MBr
14-0x13-0

Kit/Brk
10-4x
11-4

Dining
9-8x
12-6

R

Dn

vaulted

Up

Living
14-6x19-6

vaulted

Garage
21-0x19-4

First Floor

Plan #556-0270

MAPLEGLEN

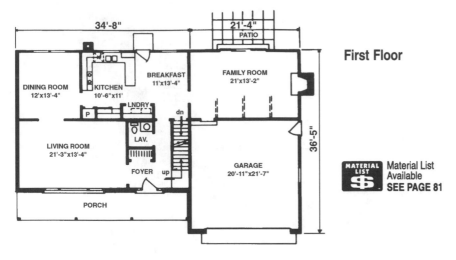

First Floor

Material List
Available
SEE PAGE 81

Second Floor - Four bedroom

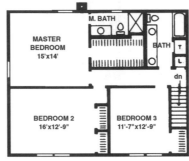

Second Floor - Three bedroom

Plan #556-T-143-1 basement
Plan #556-T-143-2 crawl space & slab

Cozy And Secluded Family Room

2,258 total square feet of living area

Special features

- Kitchen nestled between dining room and breakfast area for convenience
- Master bedroom has a large walk-in closet and private bath
- Second floor bedrooms share full bath
- 3 or 4 bedroom option, 2 1/2 baths, 2-car garage
- Basement foundation or crawl space and slab foundation drawings available, please specify when ordering
- 1,288 square feet on the first floor and 970 square feet on the second floor

Price Code D

Plan #556-N299-1 basement
Plan #556-N299-2 crawl space & slab

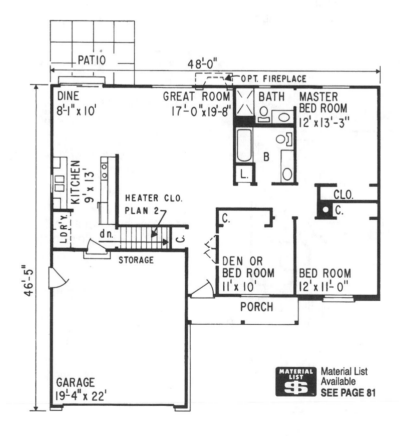

- PATIO
- 48'-0"
- O.P.T. FIREPLACE
- DINE 8'-1" x 10'
- GREAT ROOM 17'-0" x 19'-8"
- BATH
- MASTER BED ROOM 12' x 13'-3"
- B
- KITCHEN 9' x 13'
- HEATER CLO. PLAN 2
- CLO.
- C.
- L.
- LDR'Y.
- dn.
- C.
- STORAGE
- C.
- DEN OR BED ROOM 11' x 10'
- BED ROOM 12' x 11'-0"
- PORCH
- 46'-5"
- GARAGE 19'-4" x 22'

MATERIAL LIST $ Material List Available **SEE PAGE 81**

Classic Ranch With Inviting Covered Front Porch

[1,317 total square feet of living area]

Special features

- Galley-style kitchen includes access to laundry and dining area
- Dining area joined by great room creating an open atmosphere
- Lovely patio off dining area brings the outdoors in
- Well-designed laundry area nestled between garage and kitchen
- 3 bedrooms, 2 baths, 2-car garage
- Basement foundation or crawl space and slab foundation drawings available, please specify when ordering

Price Code A

PARAMOUNT

Plan #556-1270-1 basement
Plan #556-1270-2 slab

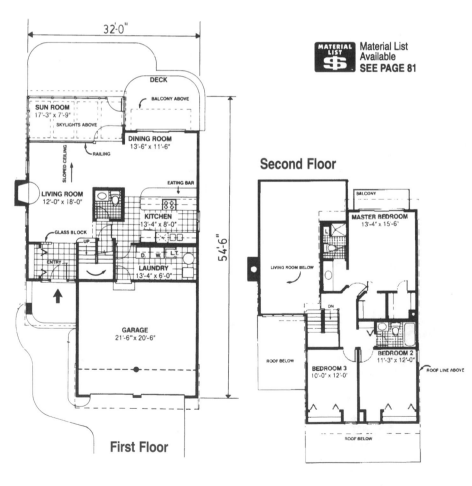

Second Floor

First Floor

MATERIAL LIST $ Material List Available SEE PAGE 81

Desirable Home For Tapered Or Narrow Lot

1,873 total square feet of living area

Special features

- Interesting contemporary roof lines
- Vaulted living room is separated from foyer by glass block wall
- Spacious sunroom with skylights adjoins living room
- Kitchen has useful breakfast bar which overlooks dining area
- Master suite has all the pleasing amenities including a balcony
- 3 bedrooms, 2 1/2 baths, 2-car garage
- Basement foundation or slab foundation drawings available, please specify when ordering
- 896 square feet on the first floor and 977 square feet on the second floor

Price Code C

Plan #556-N297-1 basement
Plan #556-N297-2 crawl space & slab

Inviting Covered Corner Entry

| 1,042 total square feet of living area |

Special features

- Living room brightened by several windows
- Spacious kitchen area includes laundry closet for washer and dryer and space for dining area
- Front entry has handy coat closet
- Plenty of extra storage space in the garage
- 2 bedrooms, 1 bath, 2-car garage
- Basement foundation or crawl space and slab foundation drawings available, please specify when ordering

Price Code AA

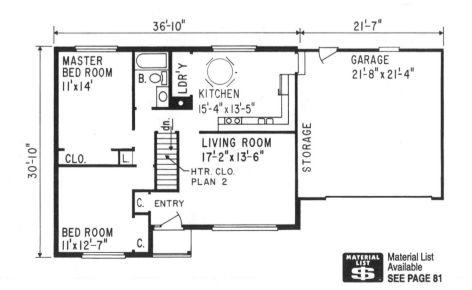

MATERIAL LIST $
Material List
Available
SEE PAGE 81

RYLAND

Classic Ranch Has Grand Appeal With Expansive Porch

1,400 total square feet of living area

Special features

- Master bedroom is secluded for privacy
- Large utility room with additional cabinet space
- Covered porch provides an outdoor seating area
- Roof dormers add great curb appeal
- Vaulted ceilings in living room and master bedroom
- Oversize 2-car garage with storage
- 3 bedrooms, 2 baths, 2-car garage
- Basement foundation, drawings also include crawl space foundation

Price Code A

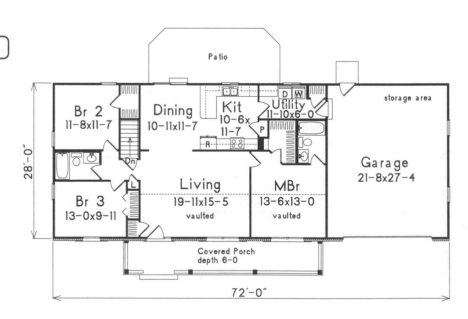

Patio

Br 2
11–8x11–7

Dining
10–11x11–7

Kit
10–6x
11–7

Utility
11–10x6–0

storage area

Garage
21–8x27–4

28'–0"

Br 3
13–0x9–11

Living
19–11x15–5
vaulted

MBr
13–6x13–0
vaulted

Covered Porch
depth 6–0

72'–0"

Plan #556-0690

PONDOSA

Plan #556-1120-1 basement
Plan #556-1120-2 crawl space & slab

Perfect Country Haven

1,232 total square feet of living area

Special features

- Ideal porch for quiet quality evenings
- Great room is opening to dining area for those large gatherings
- Functional L-shaped kitchen includes broom cabinet
- Master bedroom contains large walk-in closet and compartmented bath
- 3 bedrooms, 1 bath, optional 2-car garage
- Basement foundation or crawl space and slab foundation drawings available, please specify when ordering

Price Code A

44'-0"   PATIO optional   22'-0"

MASTER BEDROOM 11' x 13'-3"

KITCHEN 9'-3" x 13'-3"

GARAGE 21'-8" x 21'-4"

BATH

broom cabinet

optional partition

34'-0"

C L

C

rail

C

FOYER

BEDROOM 10' x 10'-3"

BEDROOM 9' x 10'-3"

GREAT ROOM 14' x 27'-3"

PORCH

MATERIAL LIST $ Material List Available **SEE PAGE 81**

PRESTON

Layout Has All The Essentials For Comfort

1,044 total square feet of living area

Special features

- Galley-style kitchen, compact yet efficient includes extra space for dining
- Living/dining area combine for added space
- Bedrooms secluded for privacy from main living areas
- Bedrooms have ample closet space
- 2 bedrooms, 1 bath, 2-car garage
- Basement foundation or crawl space and slab foundation drawings available, please specify when ordering

Price Code AA

 Material List Available
SEE PAGE 81

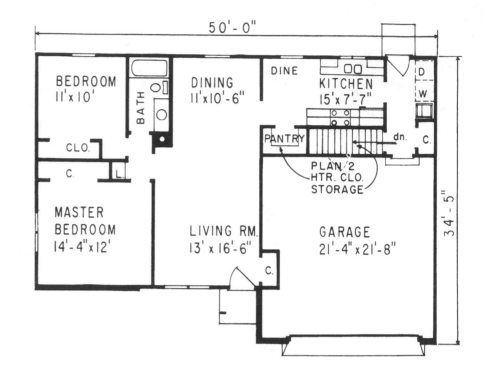

Plan #556-ES-109-1 basement
Plan #556-ES-109-2 crawl space & slab

Country-Style With Spacious Rooms

1,197 total square feet of living area

Special features

- U-shaped kitchen includes ample work space, breakfast bar, laundry area and direct access to outside
- Large living room with convenient coat closet
- Master bedroom features large walk-in closet
- 3 bedrooms, 1 bath
- Crawl space foundation, drawings also include basement and slab foundations

Price Code AA

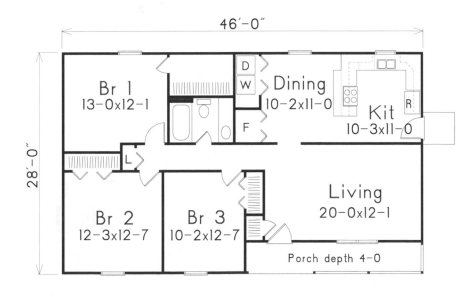

46´-0"

28´-0"

Br 1
13-0x12-1

D
W
Dining
10-2x11-0

Kit
10-3x11-0

R

F

L

Br 2
12-3x12-7

Br 3
10-2x12-7

Living
20-0x12-1

Porch depth 4-0

CUSTOMIZER KiT — Customize This Plan SEE PAGE 4

MATERIAL LIST $ — Material List Available SEE PAGE 81

Plan #556-0507

ROSEWIND

Year-Round Or Weekend Getaway Home

1,339 total square feet of living area

Special features

- Full-length covered porch enhances front facade
- Vaulted ceiling and stone fireplace add drama to family room
- Walk-in closets in bedrooms provide ample storage space
- Combined kitchen/dining area adjoins family room for perfect entertaining space
- 3 bedrooms, 2 1/2 baths
- Crawl space foundation
- 924 square feet on the first floor and 415 square feet on the second floor

Price Code A

CUSTOMIZER KiT Customize This Plan **SEE PAGE 4**

MATERIAL LIST $ Material List Available **SEE PAGE 81**

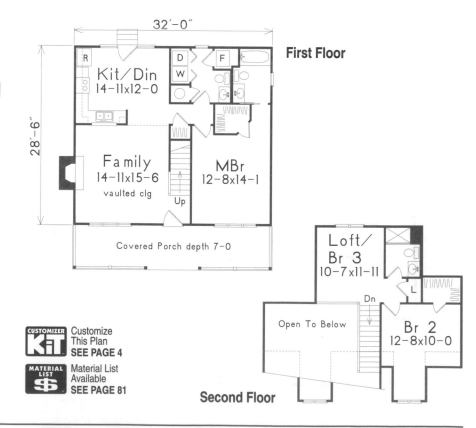

Plan #556-0692

JONESBORO

Plan #556-1189-1 basement
Plan #556-1189-2 crawl space & slab

Lovely Inviting Covered Porch

1,120 total square feet of living area

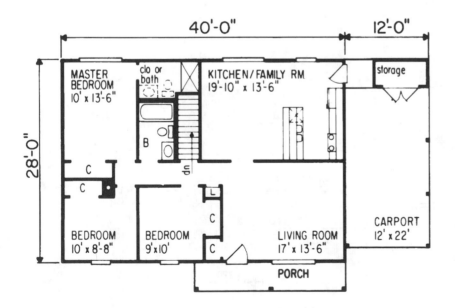

Special features

- Kitchen/family room creates a useful spacious area
- Rustic, colonial design perfect for many surroundings
- Oversized living room ideal for entertaining
- Carport includes functional storage area
- 3 bedrooms, 2 baths, 1-car carport
- Basement foundation or crawl space and slab foundation drawings available, please specify when ordering

Price Code AA

Material List Available
SEE PAGE 81

OAKTRAIL

Compact Home Maximizes Space

987 total square feet of living area

Special features

- Galley kitchen opens into the cozy breakfast room
- Convenient coat closets located by both entrances
- Dining/living room combined for expansive open area
- Breakfast room has access to the outdoors
- Front porch great for enjoying outdoor living
- 3 bedrooms, 1 bath
- Basement foundation

Price Code AA

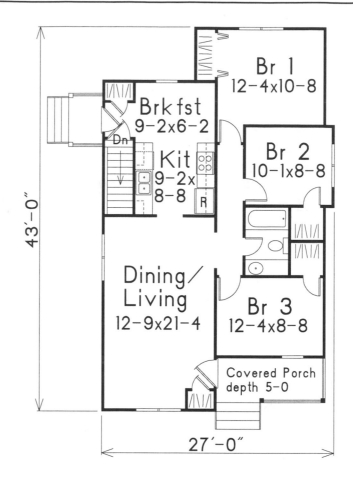

Br 1
12-4x10-8

Brk fst
9-2x6-2

Dn

Kit
9-2x
8-8

Br 2
10-1x8-8

Dining/
Living
12-9x21-4

Br 3
12-4x8-8

Covered Porch
depth 5-0

43'-0"

27'-0"

 Customize This Plan **SEE PAGE 4**   Material List Available **SEE PAGE 81**

Plan #556-0495

First Floor

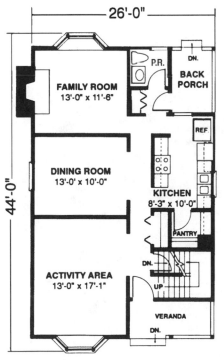

26'-0"

44'-0"

FAMILY ROOM
13'-0" x 11'-6"

P.R.

DN.

BACK PORCH

REF.

DINING ROOM
13'-0" x 10'-0"

KITCHEN
8'-3" x 10'-0"

PANTRY

ACTIVITY AREA
13'-0" x 17'-1"

DN.

UP

VERANDA

DN.

Material List Available
SEE PAGE 81

Second Floor

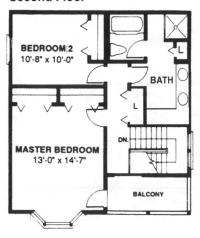

BEDROOM 2
10'-8" x 10'-0"

BATH

L

L

DN.

MASTER BEDROOM
13'-0" x 14'-7"

BALCONY

Victorian Detailing Adds Interest

1,662 total square feet of living area

Special features

- Activity area becomes ideal place for family gatherings
- Well-organized kitchen includes lots of storage space, walk-in pantry and plenty of cabinetry
- The rear of the home features a versatile back porch for dining or relaxing
- Second floor includes both bedrooms, and the master suite has a bay window and private balcony
- 2 bedrooms, 1 1/2 baths
- Basement foundation
- 1,092 square feet on the first floor and 570 square feet on the second floor

Price Code B

Plan #556-1295-1

HOLLYBRIDGE

Lovely, Spacious Floorplan

> 1,558 total square feet of living area

Special features

- Spacious utility room located conveniently between garage and kitchen/dining area
- Bedrooms separated off main living areas by hallway adds privacy
- Enormous living area with fireplace and vaulted ceilings opens to kitchen and dining area
- Master suite enhanced with large bay window, walk-in closet and private bath
- 3 bedrooms, 2 baths, 2-car garage
- Basement foundation

    Price Code B

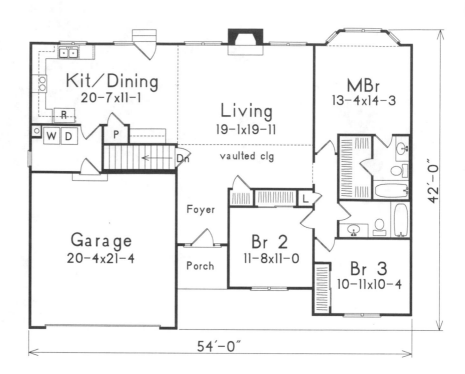

Kit/Dining 20-7x11-1

Living 19-1x19-11
vaulted clg

MBr 13-4x14-3

Garage 20-4x21-4

Foyer

Br 2 11-8x11-0

Porch

Br 3 10-11x10-4

42'-0"

54'-0"

CUSTOMIZER KIT Customize This Plan **SEE PAGE 4**

MATERIAL LIST $$ Material List Available **SEE PAGE 81**

Plan #556-0702

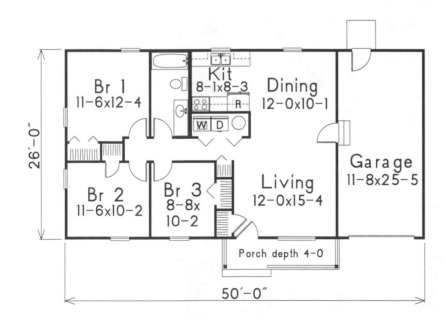

Front Porch And Center Gable Add Style To This Ranch

988 total square feet of living area

Special features

- Pleasant covered porch entry
- Living, dining and kitchen areas are combined to maximize space
- Entry has convenient coat closet
- Laundry closet is located adjacent to bedrooms
- 3 bedrooms, 1 bath, 1-car garage
- Basement foundation, drawings also include crawl space foundation

Price Code AA

CUSTOMIZER **KiT** Customize This Plan **SEE PAGE 4**

MATERIAL LIST **$** Material List Available **SEE PAGE 81**

Plan #556-0195

Our Blueprint Packages Offer...

Quality plans for building your future, with extras that provide unsurpassed value, ensure good construction and long-term enjoyment.

A quality home - one that looks good, functions well, and provides years of enjoyment - is a product of many things - design, materials, craftsmanship. But it's also the result of outstanding blueprints - the actual plans and specifications that tell the builder exactly how to build your home.

And with our BLUEPRINT PACKAGES you get the absolute best. A complete set of blueprints is available for every design in this book. These "working drawings," accompanied by our General Building Specifications, are highly detailed, resulting in two key benefits:

- *Better understanding by the contractor of how to build your home, and...*

- *More accurate construction estimates.*

When you purchase one of our designs, you'll receive all of the BLUEPRINT components shown here - elevations, foundation plan, floor plans, cross-sections, and details. Other helpful building aids are also available to help make your dream home a reality.

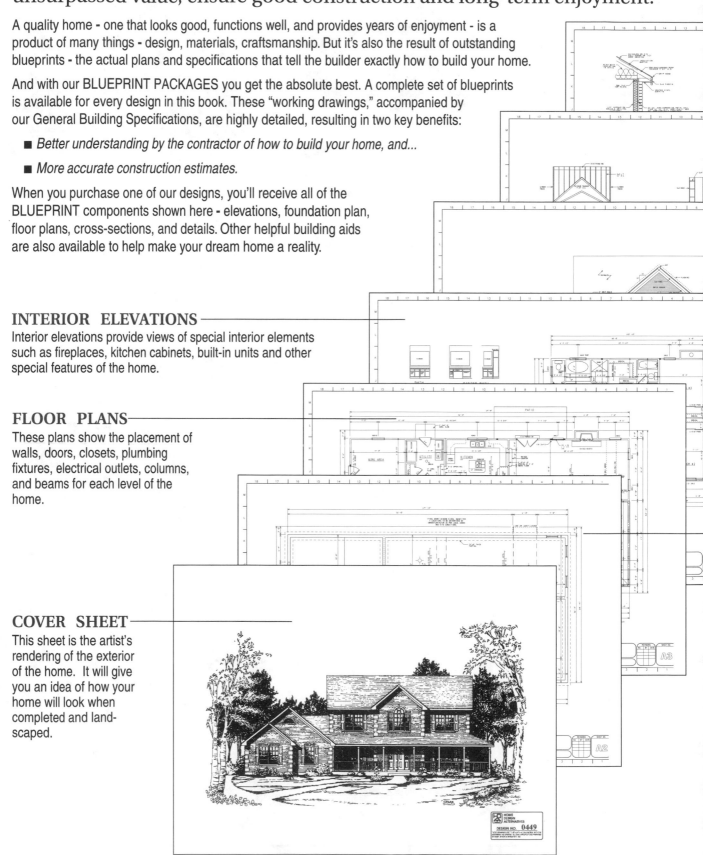

INTERIOR ELEVATIONS
Interior elevations provide views of special interior elements such as fireplaces, kitchen cabinets, built-in units and other special features of the home.

FLOOR PLANS
These plans show the placement of walls, doors, closets, plumbing fixtures, electrical outlets, columns, and beams for each level of the home.

COVER SHEET
This sheet is the artist's rendering of the exterior of the home. It will give you an idea of how your home will look when completed and land-scaped.

80

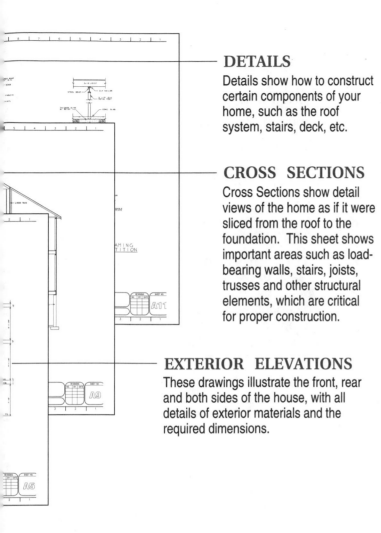

DETAILS

Details show how to construct certain components of your home, such as the roof system, stairs, deck, etc.

CROSS SECTIONS

Cross Sections show detail views of the home as if it were sliced from the roof to the foundation. This sheet shows important areas such as load-bearing walls, stairs, joists, trusses and other structural elements, which are critical for proper construction.

EXTERIOR ELEVATIONS

These drawings illustrate the front, rear and both sides of the house, with all details of exterior materials and the required dimensions.

FOUNDATION PLAN

The foundation plan shows the layout of the basement, crawlspace, slab, or pier foundation. All necessary notations and dimensions are included. See plan page for the foundation types included. If the home plan you choose does not have your desired foundation type, our Customer Service Representatives can advise you on how to customize your foundation to suit your specific needs or site conditions.

GENERAL BUILDING SPECIFICATIONS

This document outlines the technical requirements for proper construction such as the strength of materials, insulation ratings, allowable loading conditions, etc.

Other Helpful Building Aids...

Your Blueprint Package will contain all the necessary construction information to build your home. We also offer the following products and services to save you time and money in the building process.

Material List

Material lists are available for many of our plans. Each list gives you the quantity, dimensions and description of the building materials necessary to construct your home. You'll get faster and more accurate bids from your contractor and material suppliers, and you'll save money by paying for only the materials you need. Look for this **MATERIAL LIST $** symbol on the plan pages, or refer to the Home Plans Index for availability.

Customizer Kit ™

Many of the designs in this book can be customized using our exclusive Customizer Kit. It's your guide to custom designing your home. It leads you through all the essential design decisions and provides the necessary tools for you to clearly show the changes you want made. Customizer Kits are available on all designs that display this **CUSTOMIZER KIT** symbol. For more information about this exclusive product see page 4.

Rush Delivery

Most orders are processed within 24 hours of receipt. Please allow 7 working days for delivery. If you need to place a rush order, please call us by 11:00 a.m. CST and ask for overnight or second day service.

Technical Assistance

If you have questions, call our technical support line at 1-314-770-2228 between 8:00 a.m. and 5:00 p.m. CST. Whether it involves design modifications or field assistance, our designers are extremely familiar with all of our designs and will be happy to help you. We want your home to be everything you expect it to be.

 HOME DESIGN ALTERNATIVES, INC.

What Kind Of Plan Package Do You Need?

Now that you've found the home plan you've been looking for, here are some suggestions on how to make your Dream Home a reality. To get started, order the type of plans that fit your particular situation.

YOUR CHOICES:

The One-set package - This single set of blueprints is offered so you can study or review a home in greater detail. But a single set is never enough for construction and it's a copyright violation to reproduce blueprints.

The Minimum 5-set package - If you're ready to start the construction process, this 5-set package is the minimum number of blueprint sets you will need. It will require keeping close track of each set so they can be used by multiple subcontractors and tradespeople.

The Standard 8-set package - For best results in terms of cost, schedule and quality of construction, we recommend you order eight (or more) sets of blueprints. Besides one set for yourself, additional sets of blueprints will be required by your mortgage lender, local building department, general contractor and all subcontractors working on foundation, electrical, plumbing, heating/air conditioning, carpentry work, etc.

Reproducible Masters - If you wish to make some minor design changes, you'll want to order reproducible masters. These drawings contain the same information as the blueprints but are printed on erasable and reproducible paper. This will allow your builder or a local design professional to make the necessary drawing changes without the major expense of redrawing the plans. This package also allows you to print as many copies of the modified plans as you need.

Mirror Reverse Sets - Plans can be printed in mirror reverse. These plans are useful when the house would fit your site better if all the rooms were on the opposite side than shown. They are simply a mirror image of the original drawings causing the lettering and dimensions to read backwards. Therefore, when ordering mirror reverse drawings, you must purchase at least one set of right reading plans.